REVOLUTION

Volume 29

SEVEN WOMEN
AGAINST THE WORLD

SEVEN WOMEN AGAINST THE WORLD

MARGARET GOLDSMITH

LONDON AND NEW YORK

First published in 1935 by Methuen & Co. Ltd.

This edition first published in 2022
by Routledge
4 Park Square, Milton Park, Abingdon, Oxon OX14 4RN

and by Routledge
605 Third Avenue, New York, NY 10158

Routledge is an imprint of the Taylor & Francis Group, an informa business

© 1935 Margaret Goldsmith

All rights reserved. No part of this book may be reprinted or reproduced or utilised in any form or by any electronic, mechanical, or other means, now known or hereafter invented, including photocopying and recording, or in any information storage or retrieval system, without permission in writing from the publishers.

Trademark notice: Product or corporate names may be trademarks or registered trademarks, and are used only for identification and explanation without intent to infringe.

British Library Cataloguing in Publication Data
A catalogue record for this book is available from the British Library

ISBN: 978-1-032-12623-4 (Set)
ISBN: 978-1-003-26095-0 (Set) (ebk)
ISBN: 978-1-032-12995-2 (Volume 29) (hbk)
ISBN: 978-1-032-12999-0 (Volume 29) (pbk)
ISBN: 978-1-003-22716-8 (Volume 29) (ebk)

DOI: 10.4324/9781003227168

Publisher's Note
The publisher has gone to great lengths to ensure the quality of this reprint but points out that some imperfections in the original copies may be apparent.

Disclaimer
The publisher has made every effort to trace copyright holders and would welcome correspondence from those they have been unable to trace.

VERA FIGNER
1925

SEVEN WOMEN AGAINST THE WORLD

by
MARGARET GOLDSMITH

WITH A PORTRAIT

METHUEN & CO. LTD. LONDON
36 Essex Street W.C.2

First published in 1935

PRINTED IN GREAT BRITAIN

TO

THOSE WOMEN OF GERMANY

WHO ARE FIGHTING UNKNOWN
FOR HUMAN LIBERTIES

PREFACE

THE women included in this book have interested me because, so it seems to me, every one is now consciously or unconsciously concerned with revolutions and with the men and women who have made them in the past. For great social changes, or revolutions, are undoubtedly in the air, and neither the believers in these changes nor the supporters of the present order can deny that serious dislocations have occurred since the Great War in the existing system of society. Only the future can tell in whose favour the struggle for the balance of power of the various classes will be decided. It is a fact, however, that every real revolution in the past has been a step nearer the victory of the *fourth estate*.

The women revolutionaries, whose lives I have tried briefly to describe, are important not only as individuals, as heroic figures, but as an indication of this development of history in favour of the working classes. I am trying to understand the present, and that quite simply is why I have made a study of these women's careers and of the social upheavals to which they contributed.

They have also interested me for another reason : they were all fanatics, and fanaticism has been, after all, one of the greatest psychological forces of the world. Without the men and women of one idea, explorers, doctors, religious leaders, and revolution-

viii **SEVEN WOMEN AGAINST THE WORLD**

aries, there would have been no change or vitality or progress. Society would have become stagnant.

Fanatics may be difficult to absorb into everyday life ; they may be a bore as relatives or friends, but without them the world would not have become even as civilized as it is. There have, of course, been fanatics who have held up progress, who have plunged countries into wars and destruction, but perhaps historians will agree that as a whole they have had an influence for good.

Seen at close range, fanatics and cranks are often confused. It is tragic for history when fanatics are taken for cranks and are crucified, but it is equally disastrous when cranks are taken for real fanatics and are revered as such.

All the women in this book are fanatics in the best sense of the word. With one exception : Charlotte Corday, who, so it seems to me, was a crank. She has been included in this book in the hope that, in contrast to her, the heroic fanaticism of the other women will emerge more clearly.

M. G.

LONDON, *August* 10, 1935

CONTENTS

PREFACE vii

CHAP.   PAGE

I. CHARLOTTE CORDAY (1768–1793) . . . 1

II. THÉROIGNE DE MÉRICOURT (1762–1817) . . 31

III. FLORA TRISTAN (1803–1844) 67

IV. LOUISE MICHEL (1830–1905) 91

V. VERA FIGNER (1852–   ) 119

VI. EMMA GOLDMAN (1869–   ) 153

VII. ROSA LUXEMBURG (1870–1919) 183

VIII. IS THERE A REVOLUTIONARY TYPE ? . . . 217

BIBLIOGRAPHY 235

The frontispiece is reproduced from *Memoirs of a Revolutionist* by Vera Figner, by permission of Messrs. Martin Lawrence Ltd.

I

CHARLOTTE CORDAY (1768–1793)

CHARLOTTE CORDAY — Marie Anne Charlotte de Corday d'Armont before she became plain Citizen Corday—was born on July 27, 1768. She has often been idealized by biographers, because many of them have not expected women to think before they act, especially if they were young and very beautiful. ' History,' Carlyle writes of Charlotte Corday, ' will look fixedly at this one fair Apparition of Charlotte Corday ; will note whither Charlotte moves, how the little Life burns forth so radiant, then vanishes swallowed by the night.' And Lamartine, who idealizes Charlotte Corday in his *History of the Girondists*, defends her by saying that ' where there is murder, history cannot approve ; where there is heroism, history dares not condemn.'

Charlotte, as these passages indicate, has frequently been judged sentimentally rather than historically. Her tragic death has made even some serious writers assume a Scarlet-Pimpernel attitude towards the rôle she played in the French Revolution. She, with other women of the past, has been considered a great figure, because she gave everything she had, including her own life, for the cause in which she so fervently believed.

Her case shows how history has been more critical of men than of women. The cause for which women died is often put gallantly aside ; the question is evaded whether their personal and heroic sacrifices did not reflect a lack of brains ; whether, in fact, by acting emotionally and not rationally, they did not harm their particular cause more than they helped it.

2 SEVEN WOMEN AGAINST THE WORLD

Men, on the other hand, have usually been considered great only if they combined brains with character, determination, and far-sightedness, and if, apart from their fanaticism, they were rational human beings or original thinkers. In history's judgment of men, courage has not been enough, while young women like Charlotte Corday achieve lasting fame by one outstanding act of bravery.

Charlotte herself left history no doubt about her beauty. Her last request in prison before her death was that an artist be sent to paint her portrait. She was a strong woman with a beautiful complexion; her hair was brown and curly, and her face a ' perfect oval.' She had clear greyish-blue eyes, long lashes, and well-shaped eyebrows. Her chin and nose were strong, but her full lips did not look like those of a fanatic. The most attractive thing about her seems to have been her voice, which left an unforgettable impression on every one who had known or heard her.

Her contemporaries report that, despite her beauty, she lacked self-assurance. She carried herself badly, and except in her great moments she held her head so low that her chin almost touched her chest. She appeared to be vaguely ashamed of something. She blushed at the slightest provocation, and her little vanities must have been a reaction to this extreme self-consciousness. When she went out among people, she dressed with the greatest care; perhaps she was seeking moral support from a well-groomed appearance. Before she set out for Paris on the journey from which she knew she would never return, she bought a pair of smart high-heeled shoes; and in prison she prepared for her execution by throwing away her ordinary hat and making a white Normandy cap, so that she should walk up to the guillotine as ' the woman from Normandy.' She gave everything she had, and with the utmost courage, to the demands of the moment as she understood them, but she never

CHARLOTTE CORDAY

quite forgot the impression she would make on posterity.

By temperament she would never have grasped at great happiness, for she was essentially a woman who passionately desired above all to sacrifice herself, who longed to suffer so that the misery of others might be relieved. She was, in fact, the stuff of which willing martyrs have been made at any period of history. Martyrdom, Bernard Shaw once wrote in another connection, is 'the only way you can become famous without ability.'

Even had she longed for a gay, care-free existence, she would have found little happiness in her short life. In her early childhood Charlotte never knew a permanent home. She was a poor relation, frequently moved from one environment to another. Perhaps this is one reason why her mental processes remained jerky and confused to the end.

Her father was an impecunious landowner in Saint-Saturin-des-Ligneries in Normandy. He was one of those vaguely liberal aristocrats of the pre-Revolutionary era, who read the Encyclopædists, and went so far as to publish a pamphlet against the rights of primogeniture, but who remained a staunch Royalist at heart. Monsieur de Corday had a passion for helping the poor. He gave so much money and human kindness to the villagers living on his small estate Le Ronceray that little was left of either for his own children. He was extremely proud of his wife's family—she was a direct descendant of Corneille's younger sister—but this did not prevent him from carrying on continuous lawsuits with his wife's brothers. His legal activities no doubt gave him the feeling that he was doing something to provide for his growing family.

Finally, Monsieur Corday's children, whose mother seems to have been rather a shadowy figure, were sent to the homes of wealthier relatives. This

4 SEVEN WOMEN AGAINST THE WORLD

happened before Charlotte was six years old. She might have developed more naturally, become less exalted and excitable, if she had stayed longer in the peaceful country atmosphere at Le Ronceray. Until her death, however, it never occurred to her that perhaps her father should have been a more efficient provider, that perhaps he had not been quite fair to his children. On the contrary, even as a very small child she shared his passion for indiscriminate giving. Though she saw her father relatively little as she grew older, and when, years later, she lived with him again for a short time, she disagreed with him politically, she always felt the utmost respect for him. He represented male authority, and though Charlotte achieved such fame in the French Revolution, she was never a real revolutionary, and much less a rebel. ' Forgive me, my dear papa,' she wrote to her father before her death, ' for having disposed of my life without your permission.'

From the country life at Le Ronceray Charlotte was moved abruptly into an intellectual atmosphere. Her uncle, the Abbé de Corday, who was the priest in the village of Vicques, in Falaise, offered to take one of his brother's children into his home. The priest taught Charlotte how to read from a cherished old volume of Corneille, so that she should learn her letters and respect for her family at the same time. She soon became a tremendous reader, and *Polyeucte* and *Le Cid* early gave her ideas of a somewhat pompous heroism.

She was growing pathetically serious and self-controlled beyond her years. Fits of spasmodic gaiety were followed by restrained severity. She had no companions of her own age ; she never learned how to play, how to abandon herself to the joy of living. Her object in life, even at this youthful age, was to help others, to live with a purpose. Yet she never impresses one as a prig, but rather as a child who was forced into maturity. The years she spent with her uncle began to mould her into the woman, who later wrote with the utmost sincerity that 'her life had meant nothing to her whatsoever, except as it might have been useful.'

The secluded life at the vicarage caused her to regard others, who enjoyed themselves, with suspicion. The tales she heard of the pleasure-loving members of her own class would have made any serious child wonder to what this frenzy for enjoyment might lead. 'Our nation,' she once wrote in her usual exalted style, 'is too light, too trifling; it needs re-tempering, regenerating; it needs to seek in mistakes of the past the traditions of the great and the true, the beautiful and the noble; to forget all frivolities which cause the corruption and degeneration of a people.'

In view of her uncle's firm though kindly influence, it is perhaps surprising that Charlotte's inborn fanaticism did not turn to religion, the most obvious outlet for her burning wish to contribute towards the salvation of the world. There were brief périods in her life when she wanted, passionately, to take the veil, but these moods soon passed. While she was still a child she refused to accept the doctrines of the Church unquestioningly, and the Abbé de Corday complained that she 'disputed everything inch by inch, and never gave in.'

She was soon to be moved into other religious surroundings. In 1782 her father left the country and took his family to Caen, where, so he felt, he could conduct his lawsuit against his brothers-in-law more efficiently. Existence in the town, however, was harsh; there were no grateful villagers to feed his self-regard. Apart from his financial struggle, Monsieur de Corday was made unhappy by the death of his wife and his eldest child during the first few months he spent at Caen. Charlotte, whom he had

6 SEVEN WOMEN AGAINST THE WORLD

sent for as soon as he left Le Ronceray, and her elder sister Eleanore, a hunchback, kept house as best they could, and tried valiantly to keep the family together.

This time another relative, Madame de Louvagny, came to the rescue. She was a nun at the Abbaye-aux-Dames Convent at Caen, and she had heard of Monsieur de Corday's distress. This convent school, a modern establishment, was attended by the daughters of many of the French intellectual women of the eighteenth century. As a rule, boarders were not accepted, but Madame de Louvagny persuaded Madame de Belzunce, the Mother Superior, and her chief assistant, Madame de Pontecoulant, to give Charlotte and Eleanore a home. Charlotte did secretarial work for Madame de Belzunce and performed certain household duties. She made herself extremely useful. She was a poor relation no longer ; at last she was independent, she was paying for her home and her education.

At the Abbaye-aux-Dames Charlotte was as happy as a young woman of her temperament could ever have been. She was liked and appreciated by every one at the convent. For the first time in her life she had friends, and she became deeply attached to Alexandrine de Forbin. She went regularly with the nuns to visit and help the poor of the town ; she studied and read. She learned drawing and music, and, as one of her nineteenth-century biographers has expressed it, ' she became an accomplished artist both in crayons and embroidery.'

She was not always happy, however, for her adolescence brought with it attacks of morbid depression. She was often haunted by a tormenting fear of death. She was, in fact, at times so frightened of dying that speculations concerning her own future death developed into an unhealthy preoccupation.

For weeks at a time she would successfully repress these terrors. In other moods, her friends at the

Abbaye-des-Dames noticed her ‘ dreamy melancholy,’ her introspection, and her curious detachment from the problems of everyday life. Her obvious instability was not, however, given much serious thought, for, as a rule, she appeared busy and contented, fully occupied with her work and reading and with new ideas.

Democracy was in the air, and politics were freely discussed at the convent. A new and better world, passionately desired by theoretical young humanitarians like Charlotte, seemed to be looming ahead and was already reflected in the literature of the age. Raynal’s *Histoires*, which Voltaire once cruelly called ‘ rechauffé avec de la declamation,’ and which were published in Amsterdam and forbidden in France as early as 1779, made a profound impression on her. She once called Raynal her ‘ oracle,’ and his democratic doctrines moved her deeply.

She never realized that democracy could not come without a terrible social upheaval. She approached the problem emotionally ; she longed for democracy without clearly considering the issues such a change would involve. ‘ I was a Republican before the Revolution, ’ she proudly declared at her trial, but this was true only in the sense that theoretically and sentimentally she believed in the Republic. Had she been at all conscious of the cost in human life involved in establishing the new régime, she would most certainly have been unwilling to pay the price.

She was developing a passionate sense of justice, or, rather, an acute sensitiveness to injustice. The poverty she had seen in the poorer districts of Caen and elsewhere roused her anger against the existing order. The misery of others was almost unbearable to her, and she hated cruelty as much as she was incensed by violence of any kind. She was the type of reformer who, by instinct, stands up for the under-dog of the moment. The actual conflict involved in

8 SEVEN WOMEN AGAINST THE WORLD

the struggle, or even a grudging realization that the cruel fighter may ultimately bring about a decrease of misery, did not touch her mind.

Stories which reached the Abbaye-des-Dames of the luxuries indulged in by her contemporaries in Paris revolted her. She quite naturally sided with the poor, and she was reading Rousseau.

Her intense interest in the problems of the day never lessened her enthusiasm for the classics. She still worshipped the heroism of Antiquity, and she read Plutarch's *Lives* again and again. She longed to have lived in Sparta or in Rome. At the same time the convent was steeped in the Christian tradition of sacrifice, and in Charlotte's young and impressionable mind Christian sacrifice became confused with classic oratory and conspicuous acts of bravery.

When the Revolution broke out in 1789 Charlotte was still at the Abbaye-des-Dames, and there she remained for some time, as convents were not suppressed by decree until the following year. Politics, among the ladies at the convent, changed from a subject of pleasant conversation to a somewhat grimmer reality. The families of many of the nuns, and the pupils, were involved in the upheaval. Occasionally an active participant in the Revolution came to call at the convent.

A nephew of Madame de Pontecoulant, Gustave Doulcet, who was later a member of the National Convention, stayed at the convent and answered Charlotte's eager questions by the hour. He was enthusiastic about the achievements of the Revolution, and Charlotte and her fellow-students were thrilled to learn that this gallant young man had willingly renounced his titles, sacrificing them to his democratic principles. Looking back at the stirring events in France at this period, it seems almost incredible that such a gesture can have been considered impressive.

CHARLOTTE CORDAY

When the news reached Caen that on the night from the fourth to the fifth of August the Legislative Assembly had abolished all feudal rights and privileges, Charlotte rejoiced. She was convinced that the new order had begun, for—and this should never be forgotten—her sheltered existence had given her no chance to learn about life. Though she belonged to the governing class herself, she sincerely believed that the French aristocrats would willingly surrender the rights and privileges they had held for centuries without a fight.

Charlotte hated violence more than anything else in the world. It is only natural, therefore, that from the very beginning of the Revolution she supported those moderate Republicans, who later became known as the Girondists, and who came together in Madame Roland's famous salon. After the National Convention had been called in the autumn of 1792 the Girondists were bitterly attacked by the Jacobins for their non-terrorist policies.

When, at the Abbaye-des-Dames, Charlotte first began to study the Girondists' pamphlets and ideas, they were still considered radical, for they were definitely Republican, whereas many of the other deputies had not yet given up their belief in a democratic type of Monarchy.

Charlotte's faith in the peaceful coming of the new order received a violent shock late in August 1789, when the Vicomte de Belzunce, a relative of the Abbess, who had insulted the symbols of the Republic, was killed in a street riot after it became known in Caen that the Nobility and the Clergy had joined the Third Estate. To celebrate this event, a wooden pyramid, painted to look like blue marble, had been erected in a Caen street, and on it were written the words : ' Vive le Roi ! Vive Necker ! Vive les trois ordres ! '

Beside himself with rage, young Belzunce had

10 SEVEN WOMEN AGAINST THE WORLD

struck a shouting child among the enthusiastic onlookers, and as a result the mob literally tore him to bits.

It was a ghastly affair, and when Charlotte heard about it she was more shaken than she had ever been in her life before. She never quite overcame the shock this event gave her, and her horror was intensified by the inevitable realization that Belzunce's death was not really an event, but merely an unimportant incident in the Revolution as a whole. One of her conventional biographers must surely underestimate what the terrible end of a member of her immediate circle meant to her when he writes that ' she was distressed beyond measure.'

If she had been more far-sighted, more used to thinking in terms of cause and effect, the violence of the Caen crowd might have forced her to realize that her conception of a non-violent revolution was fantastic and unreal.

The Abbaye-des-Dames seemed less like a peaceful retreat after this occurrence, and Charlotte was probably glad to leave Caen when the convent was closed during the following year. She and her sister went to stay with their father. The household had already been broken up by the Revolution, an atmosphere of fear prevailed in Monsieur de Corday's home, and one of Charlotte's brothers had emigrated from France.

Monsieur de Corday was extremely nervous and less open-minded than he had been. He was changing his mind even about the rights of primogeniture. His liberalism had not stood the test of a real upheaval. Charlotte, on the other hand, was gradually forgetting, or repressing, the horror she had felt at the death of Belzunce, and her optimistic belief in an orderly establishment of a Republican régime was again asserting itself. After all, she argued with her father, the Legislative Assembly was functioning peacefully. The royal family had been escorted by a crowd back to Versailles, and Charlotte was firmly convinced that national unity had been achieved, on the sixteenth of July 1790, by the *Fête de la Federation* on the Champs de Mars.

Charlotte began to be annoyed with her father. Perhaps she was not quite sure enough in her own mind to bear his attacks on the Republic. She tried to revive his former liberal views, but he remained unconvinced, and he was often angry with her. Charlotte controlled herself, but at times the friction with her father got on her nerves. She seriously considered escaping from these conflicts by taking the veil. Convents, however, no longer existed in France, and it is doubtful whether any impulse would have been strong enough to cause her to leave the country and become an emigrée.

In the end, therefore, she simply left home and returned back to Caen. This was in June 1791. She went to stay with an active old cousin of almost eighty, Madame de Bretteville. As a child Charlotte had often stayed at Madame de Bretteville's estate at Verson, and the old lady had been consistently kind to her. Now she was living permanently at Caen, in the rue St. Jean.

Some of Charlotte's biographers have described Madame de Bretteville's home as very ' gloomy '; they think it must have been depressing for a young woman as beautiful as Charlotte to live with her old cousin. Life in the rue St. Jean does not, however, seem to have been as dreary as these writers believe, for, in so far as sociability was possible in such disturbing times, Madame de Bretteville continued to see her friends and to carry on her social life.

Charlotte had many admirers among the young men who came to Madame de Bretteville's home, but she was not interested in them. She was developing an unnatural aversion towards love and marriage. As

12 SEVEN WOMEN AGAINST THE WORLD

the Revolution progressed, her emotional capacities were increasingly absorbed by her fervent preoccupation with politics. Perhaps she would have seen political issues more clearly if she had experienced a normal emotional outlet, but she was already becoming one of those fanatics whose attachments to human beings count for nothing as compared with their complete devotion to their cause. The cause came first, and she was already shrinking from human relationships which might involve her in responsibilities. When she went to Paris, knowing that she herself would die in a very short time, there was no one whom she regretted leaving, no one in whom she felt a need to confide.

Long before psycho-analysis was invented, students of human nature attributed her fanaticism partly to the repression of more human instincts. When Ponsard's *Charlotte Corday* was first produced at the Comédie Française in 1850, a dramatic critic, Theodore de Banville, startled some of his contemporaries with the following remarks in his criticism of the play :

' If Corneille's granddaughter had been a wife and a mother, the fair young blood that surged through her brain and heart and made her mad with fanaticism would have filled her breasts with milk to nourish beautiful children like the child she kissed with tears in her eyes at the Palais Royal. . . . The angels who whispered into the ear of the heroine of Vaucouleurs were the same as those who urged Charlotte Corday to kill Marat ; they were her youth, her life, and her rebellious blood. . . . The most outrageous part of the glory and shame of these two girl martyrs was the virginity which our barbarous laws make a duty.'

It is quite obvious that Charlotte herself never experienced any conscious conflict between her political interests and her personal desires. She quite

naturally chose as her friends people who were concerned above all with politics. She was very friendly
with a young, self-educated man, Augustin Leclère,
who was Madame de Bretteville's steward and the
manager of her affairs. Leclère was a keen Republican,
who shared Charlotte's aversion to violence. He
gave her the works of Voltaire, and buoyed up her
hopes that the Revolution would finally settle down
into a peaceful development.

By 1792, however, it had become obvious, even to
optimistic provincials in Caen, that this was not to
be. The news of the King's flight and arrest at
Varennes reached Caen towards the end of June of
that year. By the autumn the growing restlessness of
the town was apparent to every one. The guillotine
was first used in Caen in November, and, as far as
Charlotte was concerned, the Revolution was coming
very close to home.

On November the fifth rioting broke out in front
of the Church of St. Jean, near Madame de Bretteville's house. The curé, who had refused to take
the oath on the new Constitution and who had
been dismissed from office as a result, courageously
announced Mass for nine o'clock in the morning.
Militant Republicans expressed their disapproval of
the priest by throwing stones and attacking his
supporters with their fists.

Rioting also broke out at Verson, near Madame
de Bretteville's estate. In a letter to a woman friend,
Charlotte has left us an account of what happened in
the village she knew so well. Charlotte's letter is
illuminating, for she describes only the horrors of the
uprising and not its causes. The Republic itself is
never mentioned, and the letter might have been
written by a staunch Royalist.

' You ask me, dear heart, what has happened at
Verson. Every conceivable abomination! About
fifty people have been beaten and had their hair cut

14 SEVEN WOMEN AGAINST THE WORLD

off, and women have been outraged. Apparently, it was only the women that they had a grudge against. Three died a few days later. The others are still ill, or at least most of them.

'On Easter Sunday the Verson people insulted one of the National Guard and even his cockade, which was the worst possible insult he could have been offered. Stormy deliberations! The administrative bodies were forced to give permission for people to leave Caen, and then the preparations for this lasted until half-past two. The people at Verson, who were informed in the morning, thought they were being fooled. Lastly, the curé had time to escape, leaving a funeral stranded in the middle of the street. You know that those who were there and were taken were the Abbé Adam and de La Ballue, Canon of the Sépulchre, the latter a stranger, and the former a young Abbé belonging to the parish. The women were the Abbé Adam's mother and the curé's sister ; the major of the parish was also taken. They were only four days in prison.

'One of the peasants was asked by the municipality whether he was a patriot or not. "Alas, yes, gentlemen," he replied, "I am. Everybody knows that I was the first to put the property of the clergy up to auction, and you know very well, gentlemen, that honest men would have nothing to do with it." I don't suppose a witty man could have given a better answer than this poor fool, and even the judges, for all their solemnity, found it difficult to repress a smile.

'What more can I tell you in order to cut short this sorry chapter? The parish immediately veered round ; it might have been a Club. They fêted the new converts, who would have set the curé free if he had come back.

'"You know the vile mob, it can change in a trice
And show hatred or love at a throw of the dice!"

CHARLOTTE CORDAY 15

' That's enough about them ! All the people you mention are in Paris. To-day the rest of our good people leave for Rouen, and we shall be almost alone. What can one expect ? Nobody is bound to do the impossible. I should have been altogether delighted to settle down in your district, especially as we are threatened with insurrection in the near future. But one can die only once, and my comfort in the midst of all these horrors is that I should be no loss to anybody unless my love for you means something to you. Perhaps you would be surprised if you could see how afraid I am ; but if you were here you would share my fears, I am sure. I could tell you nice tales about the state of our town and the excitement everywhere ! '

Charlotte was deeply distressed when she heard that, in August, the royal family had been imprisoned in the Temple. Her ambiguous attitude towards the King reflects her confusion of mind, her stubborn unwillingness to pay any real price for the Republic she claimed to support. At a farewell dinner party given by Madame de Bretteville for some friends who were leaving Caen—and it is interesting to realize that future refugees could have left the scene of the Revolution so conventionally—Charlotte refused to drink to the King's health. The guests, most of whom were Royalists, were deeply chagrined. By them Charlotte was considered a rebel. When they asked her why she would not toast Louis, who was ' so good and virtuous,' she replied in her clear, beautiful voice : ' I believe him virtuous, but a weak King cannot be a good one ; he cannot check the misfortunes of the people.'

This gesture shows how limited was her Republicanism. Danton once said of her : ' When she thought of Rome or Sparta, she was a Republican without reservations, when she thought of her own time, she could not help being critical. She was

16 SEVEN WOMEN AGAINST THE WORLD

later enraged when Marat, in reply to the Girondists' suggestion that an appeal be made to the people to save the King's life, wrote in his *Ami du Peuple* : ' I shall not believe in the Republic until the head of Louis XVI is no longer on his shoulders. . . . There will be no security, no peace, until the tyrant's head has fallen.'

The news of the September massacres of the Royalists in the Paris prisons reached Caen with a communication from the Committee of Public Safety, in which the town was informed that ' a number of ferocious conspirators detained in prison have been put to death by the people.' Their executions were called ' an act of justice indispensable for terrorizing traitors into keeping within bounds.'

Charlotte's despair when she heard the details of the Paris massacres was so overwhelming that her mind seems to have suffered from the strain. She forgot about the new order ; the Republic as such ceased to exist for her ; she could think only of the horrors about which she had been told. It is a curious fact that despite her preoccupation with violence, she was never morbidly curious. She never witnessed an execution. On the contrary, when she herself was being driven in a cart to her own execution, and the guillotine on the Place de la Republique loomed ahead, she asked the driver to step aside so that she could see it : she had never seen a guillotine before. Perhaps her agony at the thought of these horrors was all the greater, as they lived entirely in her imagination and were stimulated by her abnormal fantasies of violence.

' The most horrible things that can possibly happen,' she wrote at this time to a friend, ' lie in a future inaugurated by such happenings. . . . All these men, who should give us liberty, have killed liberty.'

Charlotte was not strong enough, either mentally

CHARLOTTE CORDAY

or morally, to face the ghastly realities of the Revolution. She refused to admit that at this stage bloodshed was unavoidable. The news of violent acts, which reached her daily, was unbearable to her, and she evaded inevitable mental conflicts by escaping into mystical conceptions ; she made herself believe that the Republic could and would be maintained without further violence. She dreamed about a peace which would soon be restored in France, though as yet her ideas of how this could be done were vague and undefined.

The word 'peace' was beginning to obsess her. 'The Second Day of the Preparation of Peace,' she heads the last long letter she wrote from prison, and the word occurs ten times in this letter. The last sentence she uttered at her trial was : 'The leader of Anarchy is now dead ; you will have peace.'

She was gradually moving away from reality into an abnormal state of detachment. One of her great friends, Bougon-Langrais, who was executed a year after her own death, and who understood her well, wished that he, too, like 'dear Charlotte, could have lulled himself to sleep with a sweet and deceptive illusion into believing that soon order and peace would be restored in his country.'

Charlotte's troubled mind was groping to find some one individual whom she could hold responsible for the violence which had occurred. It was much easier to believe that peace would be restored, if she could persuade herself that, as a whole, her countrymen hated violence and that one diabolical being alone was causing the terrible bloodshed.

It is probable that Charlotte developed an *idée fixe* about Marat after September the twenty-fifth, when the Assembly attacked him for his terroristic measures. 'The people, obedient to my voice,' Marat had defended himself, 'saved the country by

18 SEVEN WOMEN AGAINST THE WORLD

appointing themselves to the dictatorship to rid themselves of the traitors.'

Marat became Charlotte's symbol, the very essence of everything horrible. ' Striking at Marat,' she was asked at her trial, ' did you think you could remove all tyrants ? '—' Marat gone, the rest might fear,' she answered.

What she heard of his appearance stimulated her hatred, for already this was not too strong a phrase with which to describe her emotion for him. His physical ugliness made him more repulsive to her still : she was enraged when she thought of his short squat figure ; of his head, so much too large for his body, his protruding nose, his jerky, awkward movements, his skin, terribly disfigured by the disease he had caught while hiding from his pursuers in the cellars of Paris.

Charlotte would never have acknowledged Marat's sincerity. She would have denied stubbornly that he had sacrificed everything for the principles in which he believed. She forgot, if she had ever known it, that he gave up a brilliant career as a physician and a scientist for his political convictions, that he went to prison for them, and that now he was dying from a disease contracted while he was defending them. If any one had told Charlotte that Jean Paul Marat was a tortured human being, as she was herself—except that his mind was keen—she would have been roused to passionate anger.

It is difficult to say at what point Charlotte began to complete her fantasy of the situation. She had found the solution : peace. She had found the means to attain this peace : the devil, who had terrorized France—Marat—must be removed. The person who killed him would be her country's saviour.

It is generally assumed that Charlotte vaguely thought of herself as this saviour after the so-called ' affair of the thirty-first of May ' 1792, when a

CHARLOTTE CORDAY 19

refractory priest of the parish of St. Gilles was executed in Caen. By April of the following year, when the Convention attacked Marat, because he had encouraged a revolt against the Assembly, definite plans for saving France herself were maturing in her agitated mind.

A few weeks later, when Marat, through a deputation from the Commune, demanded the arrest of the Girondists, whom he considered active counter-revolutionaries, Charlotte became more resolute, but she must have experienced an agonizing conflict. Her every instinct was, after all, against violence, and yet she felt called upon to perform a murder as a sacred duty. Augustin Leclère later found a note among her papers. She had written : Will I do it ? Will I not do it ?—' Le ferai-je ? Ne le ferai-je pas ? '

When, in June, a number of Girondists, who had fled from Paris, began to arrive in Caen, Charlotte's mind was made up. Though she utterly confused the issues at stake, and though her plan was a mad one, she carried out the details of it in a completely calm and logical manner.

She decided to murder Marat at a plenary session of the Convention. The crowds, so she believed, would then kill her at once or trample her to death. She would die an unknown heroine. She sincerely believed that an anonymous act of courage would serve her cause best, but in the end, when she actually went out to kill him, she carefully pinned her baptismal certificate and her ' Address to Frenchmen ' to her clothing, so that every one would know who she was. This unconscious exhibitionism which reflects her longing to be acknowledged as a martyr is infinitely pathetic, for in her clear-sighted moments she wanted to sacrifice herself without receiving anything in return—even prestige.

The antagonistic attitude among her friends in

20 SEVEN WOMEN AGAINST THE WORLD

Caen towards Marat stimulated Charlotte's intentions. When, in May, the Convention sent two messengers to the town to bring back the Girondist refugees, Caen did not obey these orders. Instead, the two messengers were kept as hostages.

Charlotte realized that she must find some pretext for going to Paris. Already she was extremely secretive about her plan. Her old friend, Mademoiselle de Forbin, who had emigrated to Switzerland, wanted some one to interview the Minister of the Interior for her and to arrange about her pension. As Mademoiselle de Forbin's family knew Barbaroux, a prominent Girondist then in Caen, Charlotte made this an excuse to go to him and to ask him for some letters of introduction to people in Paris.

Leclère, in whom she had confided as little as she had in any one else, escorted her to the *Intendance*, where she had an appointment with Barbaroux. He willingly agreed to give her a note to his colleague Deperret, who was still in Paris. Barbaroux asked Charlotte to come back in a few days and he would have the letter ready for her. Barbaroux's attitude in this case helps one to understand why men like Marat were enraged by the Girondists, who were willing to give public money in the form of pensions to counter-revolutionary Royalists living abroad.

On the next Sunday, it was the seventh of July, Charlotte dressed with great care and went to see the parade General Wimppfen had arranged in the hope of raising volunteers for a march on Paris. The demonstration was a failure, for only seventeen men stepped forward. Charlotte was deeply disappointed, but her manner was as calm and restrained as ever. She walked from the parade to Barbaroux's to fetch her letter of introduction. Then she went home, for Madame de Bretteville had asked some of the Girondists to spend the evening with her.

One of the guests spoke of Charlotte as ' the

CHARLOTTE CORDAY

beautiful aristocrat, who had come in to see the Republicans.' For the first time Charlotte's composure was slightly shaken, and she answered somewhat sharply : ' You are judging me without knowing me, Citizen. One day you will know who I am.'

She was particularly casual the next day. She told Madame de Bretteville and her friends that she was going to Argentan, where her father was living. To him she wrote that she was going to England.

She went out to Verson to say good-bye to an old friend ; she returned some books to Madame de Pontecoulant, who was still living in Caen. She bought the high-heeled shoes for her journey and mended her clothes ; she reserved her place in the coach to Paris. No one could possibly have suspected that she was starting forth on her last adventure.

She left for Paris the next day. In the coach a stranger was unpleasantly attentive to her and, in the end, proposed to her. She appeared to be a young woman travelling purely for pleasure or, at most, on some trivial matter of business. She was apparently undisturbed by the thought that, a week from that very day, she would perhaps no longer be at liberty or even alive. During the night, this ' astonishing woman,' as Madame Roland once called her, slept soundly and well. ' The murmured plaintive ditties ' of her would-be admirer, as she herself admitted in a letter written shortly before her death, ' were extremely soporific,' and ' she woke up only on reaching Paris.'

She had never been in Paris, but she was not at a loss. She did not seem like a provincial. She walked into the Hôtel de la Providence, in the rue des Vieux Augustins, as though she had stayed alone at hotels many times before. At the hotel, however, upsetting news awaited her, for the waiter told her that Marat was too ill to attend the Convention. She would not be able to kill him at a plenary session. Her plans would have to be changed.

22 SEVEN WOMEN AGAINST THE WORLD

The following day she went to Deperret's home to present her letter, but he was out. She returned, and he promised to go with her the next day to see the Minister. She then returned to the hotel, went to bed, and slept well.

The next morning Deperret took her to the Ministry, where she bought a knife with which to kill Marat, warned Deperret not to be seen with her too much, found out Marat's address, wrote to him asking for an interview, and went back to the hotel to write her exalted ' Address to Frenchmen.' She was quiet and unhurried ; judging by her manner, none of these actions was more important to her than others. She would have given any one the impression that they were all in the day's routine.

Her ' Address,' however, reflects her exaltation, her intense and abnormal excitement. ' Oh, France,' she wrote, ' your peace depends upon the maintenance of the Law. I shall not offend the Law by killing Marat, for he is condemned by the Universe ; he is outside the Law. . . . Oh, my country, your miseries break my heart. I have nothing to offer you but my life, and I thank heaven that I am free to dispose of it as I will. . . .'

Marat was living in the rue des Cordelier where his devoted friend Simmone Evrard was taking care of him. As a physician he was fully aware that he had entered upon the last phase of his painful and incurable disease. He was a dying man, and Charlotte's sacrifice becomes all the more tragic, all the more meaningless, when one bears this fact in mind.

Marat was too ill to go to the Convention ; he was free from pain only when, seated in a bathtub, he wrapped his body in wet towels. His energy, his will to save the Republic were, however, as dominating as ever. He still supervised the publication of his newspaper, *Le Journal de le République Française,* which had succeeded his *Ami du Peuple* after the proclamation of the Republic.

One day in July he received a letter in an unknown handwriting. ' Citizen, I have just arrived from Caen,' he read. ' Your love for your native place will doubtless make you desirous to learn about the events which have occurred in that district of the Republic. I shall call at your home in about an hour ; have the goodness to receive me, and give me a short interview. I shall enable you to render France a great service.'

Marat, who was fighting the Girondists as bitterly as ever, must have been interested in any news from Caen, but despite this fact—perhaps he felt too ill— he obviously gave no orders that the signer of this letter was to be admitted to his house. For Charlotte was turned away when she called. She wrote once more and called again, but in vain. Finally, on the thirteenth of July, she was admitted.

At about half-past seven in the evening of that day Marat was seated in his bathtub. A board was laid across it, and on this he was writing. A young man named Pillet came in with samples of newsprint paper. Marat approved the paper, and asked the youth to open the window before leaving.

When Pillet left the house, so he later stated, he saw a handsome young woman arguing at the door with the concièrge. It was very hot, and the young woman was telling the concièrge that despite the heat she had come from Caen to see the ' Friend of the People.' Then Simmone Evrard joined the two women at the door and asked Charlotte to come in. Simmone took her up to Marat's room.

Charlotte was with Marat for about ten minutes. No one else was in the room, but she herself said at her trial that she had talked to him about the Girondists at Caen. He asked her for the names of the Girondist refugees who were then in that city. In the middle

24 SEVEN WOMEN AGAINST THE WORLD

of their conversation Charlotte drew the knife she had bought from the folds of her dress and stabbed him. She was a strong woman who aimed well despite her casual manner. She had struck into his heart, and after one cry for help Marat died.

The room was full of people almost in an instant. We are told that Charlotte seemed shaken for a moment when she witnessed Simmone Evrard's grief, but Charlotte controlled her agitation almost at once. She was far more obviously distressed when, after she had been arrested and her hands tied behind her back, her clothing was searched for any documents which might incriminate possible accomplices. At her execution, too, she appeared to be disturbed only when the scarf was pulled off her neck and shoulders. Then her acute sense of modesty was outraged.

She was taken from Marat's house to the Abbaye prison. She spent the first day there mending the frock which had been torn when she was arrested. She also asked the warder of the prison for material to make the Normandy cap. She was equally busy the next day, writing letters. To Barbaroux she wrote :

' . . . It was through the lady who travelled with me that they found out I knew you and that I had spoken to Duperret. You know how resolute Duperret is ; he told them the exact truth in answer to their questions. I confirmed his evidence by my own. There is nothing against him, but his resolution was regarded as a crime. I confess I was very much afraid they would find out I had spoken to him. I regretted having done so when it was too late, and I tried to make up for my mistake by making him promise to join you. But he was too obstinate to make any such promise. Knowing that he and everybody else were innocent, I determined to carry out my plan.

' Can you believe it, Fauchet is in prison for

CHARLOTTE CORDAY

being my accomplice, Fauchet who did not even know of my existence ! But they don't like having only an insignificant woman to offer to the shade of that great man ! Pardon me, ye men, the word is an insult to your kind ! He was a ravening monster, who would have devoured the whole of France through civil war. But now, *vive la paix !* Thank God, he was not a Frenchman born. Four of the members were present at my first examination. Chabot looked like a madman. Legendre insisted that he had seen me in the morning at his house. I never gave this man a thought. I do not think he is great enough to be the tyrant of this country, and I had no wish to punish so many people. All those who have never set eyes on me before said they had known me for a long time.

' I hear that Marat's last words have been printed. I don't know that he ever gave utterance to any ; at all events I can tell you what were the last words he said to me. After writing down the names of all of you, and the names of the members of the Calvados Government who are at Evreux, he said, to console me, that in a few days he would have you all guillotined in Paris. These last words decided his fate. If the Department sets up his bust opposite St. Fargeau's, it ought to have these words engraved in letters of gold.

' I shall not tell you any details about the great event. The newspapers will tell you all about that. I confess that what finally decided me was the courage with which our volunteers enlisted on the seventh of July. You remember how happy I was, and I promised myself that I would make Pétition regret the suspicions he harboured with regard to my feelings. " Would you be sorry if they did not go ? " he asked me. In short, I came to the conclusion that it was foolish for so many brave men to die for the head of one man whom they might miss or who might drag

26 SEVEN WOMEN AGAINST THE WORLD

down a number of worthy citizens with him. He did not deserve the honour. A woman's hand was enough. I confess that I made use of a treacherous trick to induce him to receive me ; but the end justifies the means in such circumstances.

'When I left Caen, I counted upon sacrificing him on the summit of the Mountain ; but he was no longer attending the Convention. I wish I had kept your letter ; then they would have been convinced that I had no accomplices. But all that will be cleared up. We are such good Republicans in Paris that nobody can believe that a futile woman, who would never have been of any use however long she lived, could possibly sacrifice herself in cold blood to save her country. I was expecting to die at any moment, but brave men who are really above all praise saved me from the excusable fury of those whom I had made miserable. As I really acted in cold blood, the crying of some women upset me. But if one saves one's country one must not think of the price that has to be paid.

'May Peace be established as quickly as I hope it will. An important step has been taken in that direction without which we should never have had it. I have been revelling in Peace for the last two days ; my country's good is my own. The reward for every act of devotion is far greater than the pain one feels in deciding to perform it. I am afraid they may worry my father a little ; he already has quite sufficient cause for distress in losing me. If any of my letters are found in his possession, most of them are portraits of you. If they contain any jokes at your expense, I beg you to overlook them. I gave way to the frivolity of my nature. In my last letter I led them to believe that I was terrified at the horrors of civil war, and was going to England. At that time my idea was to remain unknown, to kill Marat publicly and be killed myself at once, leaving the

CHARLOTTE CORDAY 27

people of Paris to make a vain search to discover who I was.

' I beg you, Citizen, you and your colleagues, to take up the cudgels on behalf of my relatives and friends if they are molested. I say nothing to my dear aristocratic friends whose memory I keep in my heart. I have hated only one person in my life, and I have proved the strength of my hatred. But there are thousands whom I love more than I hated him. A lively imagination and a tender heart gave promise of a stormy life, and I beg those who may possibly regret me to remember this, and rejoice to see me enjoying my rest in the Elysian Fields with Brutus and the other heroes of old.

' Among moderns there are few true patriots who know how to die for their country ; selfishness accounts for nearly everything. What a sorry people to found a Republic ! But at least the foundations of Peace must be laid, and the Government will follow as best it can. At all events, the Mountain will certainly not rule France ; you may take my word for that !

' I am treated with the utmost consideration in prison ; the concièrges are the best and kindest of souls. I have been given some gendarmes to prevent me from being bored ; that was all right during the day, but at night it is extremely disagreeable. I complained of the indecency, but the Committee did not think fit to pay any attention. I think it was Chabot's idea ; only a Capuchin could have thought of such a thing ! I while away the time writing songs. I give Valady's couplet to anybody who wants it. I have assured the people of Paris that we are taking up arms only against anarchy, which is absolutely true.

" I have been transferred to the Conciergerie, and the gentlemen of the Grand Jury have promised to send you my letter ; so I am continuing it. I have

28 SEVEN WOMEN AGAINST THE WORLD

undergone a long examination ; please get it if it is published. At the time of my arrest I had an Address on me which I had written to the Friends of Peace. I cannot send it to you. I shall ask for it to be published, though I expect it will be useless.

' I had an idea last night of presenting my portrait to the department of Calvados, but the Committee of Public Safety, to whom I addressed my request, have not answered, and now it is too late.

' It is astonishing that the people allowed me to be transferred from the Abbaye to the Conciergerie. It affords fresh proof of their attitude. Tell the good people of Caen this. They occasionally allow themselves the luxury of a little insurrection, which is not easy to keep in hand.

' To-morrow at eight o'clock my trial begins. Probably by midday I shall have lived—to use a Latin expression. People must believe in the valour of the men of Calvados since even the women of the district are capable of determinations. I have no idea how my last moments will be spent, and it is the end that crowns the achievement. There is no need for me to feign indifference to my fate, for up to the present I have not felt the smallest fear of death. I never had any regard for life except as a means of being useful.

.   .   .   .

' I hope you will not cease to take an interest in Madame Forbin's business. This is her address if you find it necessary to write to her : Alexandrine Forbin, Mandresie, near Zürich, Switzerland. I beg you to tell her that I love her with all my heart.

' I am going to write a word to my father ; I shall not say anything to our other friends. All I ask of them is to forget me quickly ; their grief would disgrace my memory. Tell General Wimpffen that I believe I have helped him to win more than one battle by paving the way to peace.

CHARLOTTE CORDAY

'Farewell, Citizen! I commend myself to the memory of the true Friends of Peace.

'The prisoners in the Conciergerie, far from insulting me like the people in the streets, looked as though they pitied me. Misfortune always arouses sympathy. This is my last reflection.

'Tuesday the sixteenth, at eight o'clock in the evening. 'CORDAY.'

That evening she also wrote to the Committee of Public Safety, and as a result Jean Jacques Hauer was sent to make a hurried portrait of her.

'As I still have a few hours to live' (she had written to the Committee), 'may I be allowed to hope, Citizens, that you will allow me to have my portrait painted? I should like to leave it as a memento to my friends. Moreover, just as the likeness of good citizens are cherished and held in honour, so curiosity may sometimes lead to a desire to know what great criminals looked like, since this would serve to perpetuate the horror felt for their crimes. If you deign to heed my request, I beg you to send me a miniature painter to-morrow. I take this opportunity of repeating the request that I may sleep alone. Assuring you of my deepest gratitude. 'CHARLOTTE CORDAY.'

On the sixteenth of July Charlotte was tried by the Revolutionary Tribunal. Two developments at the trial were extremely painful to her. In the first place, the Tribunal could not believe that she had killed Marat without powerful accomplices, that she alone, and with no confidant whatsoever, had carried out this murder. She, who had longed passionately to be the saviour of France, was accused of being merely the instrument of influential men.

Secondly, the judge, who was moved by her youth, urged her defending counsel to plead that she

30 SEVEN WOMEN AGAINST THE WORLD

was mad. She vehemently rejected this suggestion. Had he succeeded, her deed, in her own eyes, would have been utterly futile. Nor would she have attained the height of exaltation towards which she was moving; she might have been pardoned and she would not have died, thus sacrificing herself for the cause of peace. Her whole life would have become meaningless to her. ' I killed a man in order to save thousands,' she said proudly at the trial.

Charlotte was executed in the late afternoon of the day of her trial, July 17, 1793. She was not quite twenty-five years old. It never occurred to her that her death might not bring peace to France—the fact that, historically speaking, the giving of her life meant nothing at all, never crossed her mind. And if she was afraid of dying, if, as the cart approached the guillotine, she felt regret for what she had done or at leaving life, she did not show her fear. Her self-control, her poise, her calm were perfect to the end. As Pierre Vergniaud, who had so strenuously opposed the institution of the Revolutionary Tribunal which had sentenced her to death, said of Charlotte and of Madame Roland : ' These women, if they cannot deliver us, can teach us how to die.'

II

THÉROIGNE DE MÉRICOURT (1762–1817)

THÉROIGNE DE MÉRICOURT'S life was so frivolous before the French Revolution, when her emotions were centred on politics, that it is difficult to disentangle the maze of facts and fiction which has been handed down to us about her. Puritanical historians, with a fondness for heroines who are as pure as they are resolute and beautiful, have been extremely discreet about her, claiming that the tales of her adventurous youth are an invention, or at best malicious gossip. Some of her more romantic biographers, on the other hand, eager to crowd as much passion as possible into their accounts of her, have snatched at every record of an intriguing rumour which was spread about her while she was alive.

Anne-Josèphe Terwaine or Terwagne, which later became the more euphonious French Théroigne, was born on August 13, 1762, in the village of Marcourt, on the river Outhe in Luxembourg. Later, when she developed a passion for high-sounding names, she added the de Méricourt to her own. She loved assumed names, and sometimes she called herself Madame de Campinados, after a town where her brother then lived. Once, when she was in England, the word 'Spinster' was added to her signature on a deed, and there were people—who did not know English—who thought that she was Miss Spinster. To history she is best known as 'La belle Liègeoise,' for the village of her birth was not far from Liège.

Anne-Josèphe was the oldest of four children, and she was the only daughter in the family. Her father, Peter Théroigne, was a prosperous farmer until he

32 SEVEN WOMEN AGAINST THE WORLD

yielded to his insatiable desire for risky business speculations. He was a quick-tempered man who loved lawsuits. He usually lost these, so that they became an expensive hobby.

According to rumour, he tried to improve his distressing financial situation by allowing an old German aristocrat, a Baron Clootz, to support Anne-Josèphe—and the rest of the family—when she was twelve years old. This is, however, undoubtedly a legend, for Théroigne was independent from the time when she was a very young girl. She was headstrong and unstable, her judgment of people was often wrong, but she never accepted any one's advice about her personal relationships, and consistently, throughout her life, she chose her own intimates.

Her youth was stormy. Her mother died when she was eleven, and as her father planned to marry again, Anne-Josèphe was sent to live with an aunt at Liège, where she attended a convent school. This was the only formal education this remarkable woman ever had, for after she had been in Liège for a year, her aunt remarried and felt that she could no longer pay for the child's schooling. Anne-Josèphe remained at her aunt's, but from now on she became a maid of all work in the home.

Refusing to accept this situation, she left Liège and returned to her father. She found a stepmother who was as harsh as her aunt had been. So she and her two brothers ran away from home. They went to Germany, and Anne-Josèphe, who was thirteen, tried her luck in the home of some other relatives, who lived in Sougne, in Luxembourg. Here she was given the task of herding cows. She stayed for a year. Then, bored with this work, she returned to Liège and learned dressmaking.

She was not a dressmaker for long. In Liège she met a woman who took her to Antwerp as a nurse for her child. It is not known whether Anne-Josèphe

THÉROIGNE DE MÉRICOURT 33

was inefficient or not, but when they reached Antwerp her employer suddenly dismissed her. Young Anne-Josèphe, however, was quite equal to the difficult situation of being stranded in a strange city with no money and no work.

She immediately looked for and found another post. An English lady, Mrs. Colbert, struck by the girl's unusual personality, engaged her as a governess for her child. Anne-Josèphe lived with this family for four years. They spent most of the time in Antwerp, but with Mrs. Colbert she also travelled. She saw Brussels, and she lived for months at a time in London. Above all, Mrs. Colbert gave her an opportunity of studying music and taking singing lessons.

On one of her visits to London—this was in 1782, when she was twenty—Anne-Josèphe fell in love. The young Englishman's name is not known. He persuaded her to elope with him, but he could not marry her without his parents' consent. She lived with this youth for three years, and there was much talk of marriage when at last he would be of age. But when this happened and he inherited a fortune, he was less enthusiastic about a permanent relationship. In 1785 he took her to Paris and left her there, after supplying her most generously with money.

The de Goncourt brothers, who did a great deal of research on Théroigne's history, record that in Paris she soon found another protector, a prominent and wealthy parliamentary Councillor, Doublet de Persan. He arranged for her to have musical training, and she sang in Paris concerts. She appears to have had a sincere passion for music—as well as for musicians—and she was known in Paris as a regular attendant of concerts and the opera.

Comte Thomas d'Espinchal, who wrote a *Journal de Voyage et de Faits relatifs à la Révolution*, mentions

3

34 SEVEN WOMEN AGAINST THE WORLD

her in his book. ' Persons like myself,' he writes, ' who used to frequent the theatres and other public places before 1789, can remember that only a few years before there often appeared at the opera, and even more frequently at the Spiritual Concerts, alone in a prominent box, a fair unknown who called herself Madame Campinados. She wore many diamonds, she had her own carriage, she came from a foreign country. She appeared to be a *fille entretenue*, but she gave no account of the resources at her disposal. This was the same person who, after the Revolution began, appeared under the name of Mademoiselle Théroigne de Méricourt.'

Though, as this passage shows, de Persan was obviously very much attached to her, she was often seen with Giacomo Davide, a famous Italian singer of the period. He took part in the religious concerts, the *concerts spirituels*, first organized by Louis XV, and the Salles des Suisses of the Tuileries was crowded whenever Davide appeared.

Davide was not the only famous singer in whom she was interested. In 1785 she decided that she wanted to go to London for a visit. It is not known whether she was feeling slightly bored with de Persan or whether, as she assured him, she was going ' to devote herself entirely to Art.' At any rate she went.

She chose as her singing master Tenducci, who had a great vogue at Covent Garden in the 'seventies and 'eighties of the eighteenth century. Many years before he had been involved in a notorious scandal, when an Irish heiress had eloped with him. When Théroigne met him he was fifty, and not in the least attractive to most women. ' In spite of his age and his ugliness,' a contemporary reports, ' and his still more hideous character, Tenducci was very keen about our illustrious Comtesse de Campinados.'

For several years Théroigne was completely under this man's influence. He persuaded her to sign an

THÉROIGNE DE MÉRICOURT 35

agreement with him, whereby he gave her singing
lessons for eight shillings instead of half a guinea, but
in return she seems to have pledged herself to do
everything he wanted.

' It was a false agreement in all its clauses,' she
writes in her *Confessions*, ' and I was foolish enough to
sign it without having it read over to me and explained.
Amongst other things there was a clause relating to a
forfeit of a thousand louis if I failed to carry out my
part of the contract, and other conditions which
utterly revolted me when at length I had the contract
read and explained to me for the first time in Italy.
There was even a clause that I should sing at the
theatre, which was a lie, as it would have been easy
for me to prove.'

Before Théroigne had been disillusioned about
him she brought Tenducci back to Paris and then
went with him to Italy late in 1787. She remained in
Genoa with the Italian for over a year. There is no
question that he tried to exploit her in every way, but
his life, too, cannot have been easy. For Théroigne,
about whom some one once said, ' love me, love my
brothers,' had brought all three of them with her, and
they shared her home with Tenducci.

' I came to Italy to sing and to study,' she wrote to
a financier named Perregaux, who often helped her.
' I brought my three brothers with me. One of them
is studying painting, and the other two are studying for
commercial careers. As I am obliged to travel, I wish
to establish the eldest at Liège, where we have relatives
who are in business. I need three thousand livres,
or three thousand five hundred, in order to purchase
a managership for my eldest brother, so that the income
derived from this sum will suffice for his needs while
he is still apprenticed in an office.'

This letter casts a gloom of realism on Carlyle's
gallant defence of Théroigne when he attributes the
tales of her wealth to ' Calumnious Royalism,' and

36 SEVEN WOMEN AGAINST THE WORLD

when he says that she ' had only the limited earnings of her profession of unfortunate-female ; money she had not, but brown locks, the figure of a heathen goddess, and an eloquent tongue and heart.'

It is not known whether she got the particular amount from Perregaux or not, but the note reflects her conviction that the world in general, and men in particular, owed her a living and a very good one. Her wanderings in Europe had not made her think that de Persan's responsibilities towards her had ceased. On the contrary, she wrote to him whenever she was in financial difficulties. One of his letters to her, written while she was in Italy, shows how completely self-centred she was. Nor did she ever feel grateful to him. At her trial in Austria, when she was asked about the companions of her youth, she remarked about de Persan : ' What did the old man matter to me ? I hate the very thought of him.'

' My sentiments towards you,' he wrote to her when she had gone to Italy with Tenducci, ' will never change, and can you in turn say that you have anything to complain about in my conduct ? It is true that I could not come to see you before you left Paris. Two reasons prevented me from doing so. Business was the first, but secondly, I knew that I had very little influence on you. When you left for England it was to be for two months. You remained there for six. When you returned to France I realized that you still had the same passion for music. You were involved with a musician with whom you intended to go to Spain. From Paris you went to your own province. After that you wanted to go to Italy. Does all this express the slightest feeling of friendship and gratitude towards me ? It was only with difficulty that I saw you alone even for a quarter of an hour. I foresaw what would happen with your music-master. You always treated me badly, though I never showed you anything but kindness, and you were always taken in by all the Italians and foreigners with whom you made friends.

‘ You were right to tell me about yourself and your family. No one will ever take a greater interest in them than I do. If you are under the impression that I neglected you, you must let me know as soon as your season at Genoa ends. You will have learned by then how the man who has sworn to love you for ever will have carried out his bargain. What did you tell me when you went to England ? That it would not interfere with our friendship. But when you returned to France, I am informed that you had entered into an engagement for five years. Have you ever kept a single promise to me ? Tell me which of us has the right to complain of the other ? Yes, chère amie, you have been very unkind both to my purse and to my heart.

‘ Farewell, my dear. Count on the sentiments with which you have inspired me, and which, despite the wrong you have done me, will end only with the death of him who will love and honour you always.’

When, in 1789, Théroigne first heard of the growing social unrest in Paris she suddenly remembered that she came of peasant stock, that she belonged to the Third Estate. She became an ardent revolutionary over-night, as it were, changing from a self-centred adventuress into a woman, who, though she understood little of what was happening, was yet deeply moved by the great events of her age. Whatever her life was like before the Revolution, there is no question of her sincerity after it began, and it seems as unkind as it is unjust for Stefan Zweig, in his *Marie Antoinette*, to state that the ‘ women crowded into the meeting hall of the National Assembly to sleep there—except for a few of them, professional prostitutes (of whom Théroigne de Méricourt was one) ’. Her sudden conversion to a socially minded creature does, however, reflect her lack of mental

38 SEVEN WOMEN AGAINST THE WORLD

balance, an unstableness which later developed into that tragic insanity which clouded the second half of her life.

She returned to Paris on the eleventh of May 1789, six days after the States-General had convened in Versailles, that is to say, historically speaking, six days after the French Revolution had begun.

That is how we classify this event, now that the Revolution stands out clearly as an historic occurrence, as the beginning of a new era in world history. Many Frenchmen, dissatisfied with the régime though they were, had not, of course, the slightest perception of what the sum of their individual discontents would ultimately mean to France and to Europe.

Louis XVI, too, remained naïve. 'You are bringing me the news of a revolt,' he said anxiously to the messenger who came to Versailles to tell him that the Bastille had fallen. And the King was taken aback when the messenger answered : 'No, Sire, it is a Revolution.'

It is not surprising, therefore, that many foreigners who were in Paris during this momentous spring and summer interpreted the restlessness of the population as a lively political period but nothing more. Very few documents reflect this unsuspecting attitude more clearly than the letters which an Englishman, Dr. Edward Rigby, a Lancashire physician who was travelling for pleasure in France with two friends, wrote to his family. His letter reminds one of Stendhal's young hero in the *Chartreuse de Parme*, who asks the vivandière what the excitement is about and whether there has been a battle, and of her answer : 'Yes, this is Waterloo ; there was a battle of sorts.'

'We have now seen enough of Paris,' Dr Rigby writes, 'to be convinced that it is not that dirty, ill-built, inconvenient place which our ill-tempered countrymen have described it. There are more magnificent buildings than in London ; all the places

THÉROIGNE DE MÉRICOURT 39

worth seeing are also more accessible than in London ;
it costs less to be admitted, and many may be seen
without paying anything. The people, too, are very
communicative. I own I am disposed to think very
highly of this people.'

Then almost in surprise, at any rate quite casually,
without a paragraph to emphasize his next remark,
Dr Rigby continues : ' Every one is talking politics.
Papers are sold at the corners of the streets, and large
parties are constantly in the Palais Royal earnestly
talking. *Les Tiers États* is the popular cry. In the
morning our carriage was stopped by some men who
were paving the street. On looking in, they said:
" Laissez-les passer ; ils sont Monsieurs des Tiers
Etats." We are to go to Versailles in a few days,
where we expect to hear the debates in the National
Assembly, which will be a great gratification at so
very important a period. After seeing Notre Dame,
we visited the Arsenal, but could not get permission
to see the Place d'Armes. The celebrated Monsieur
Lavoisier lives in a handsome hotel near. I had a
letter to him from Dr. Priestley, but he was engaged
on urgent business. In the arsenal nitre is purified
for gunpowder, under the direction of Monsieur
Lavoisier. We saw some beautiful crystals of nitre.
We thence went to the manufacturing of plate glass,
which is a most extensive business. We saw plates
of very large size, and the application with tin the
same as in England, but, being on a larger scale, it
seems to be done with more accuracy. We also saw
the Bastille, a formidable building. We dined at a
table d'hôte and had an excellent dinner, with wine
and fruit, at 1s. 8d. each. In the evening we went
again to the Theatre Italien, and saw Madame de
Gazon in the *Barbe Bleu*. It was altogether a fine
specimen of the bad taste of the French drama ; but
Madame de Gazon has certainly great power and a
fine voice. She managed to shriek, on opening the

40 SEVEN WOMEN AGAINST THE WORLD

closet door and seeing her predecessors hanging, admirably well. We supped with Mr. Dallas, and walked in the Palais Royal between eleven and twelve ; it was full of people, agitated and talking politics. . . . We are all perfectly well, and have found no inconvenience of any kind since we left England, except bugs, of which my companions complain, but I have escaped entirely.'

This letter was written five days before the fall of the Bastille, and, as it shows, Théroigne's immediate surroundings, too, were relatively calm. In the Hôtel de Toulouse, where she took a room, the routine of the day had not been interrupted. There was much excited talk, but her meals were served to her punctually and regularly. She devoted much of her time to her music and to talking to people who returned to the hotel after witnessing agitated crowds in the streets. Théroigne was still an observer.

Soon, however, she became more and more interested in the political significance of events. Instead of waiting to hear the latest news from her fellow-lodgers at the hotel, she began to walk about the city herself. She was profoundly moved and happy when, on June 17, the Third Estate, now unable to obtain the co-operation of the other two Estates— the clergy and the aristocracy—declared itself to be the National Assembly. She did not fully understand the political implications of this decision, but ' gradually a light dawned upon her and she realized clearly the position of the people as opposed to that of the privileged classes.' Her feeling of solidarity with the masses grew more intense ; she studied the developments leading up to the revolt of the Third Estate.

On July 12, the day after Necker's dismissal, Théroigne joined the crowd of people assembled in the Palais Royal Gardens to hear Camille Desmoulins' impassioned speech calling them to arms. When the huge crowd listening to him tore the leaves from the

THÉROIGNE DE MÉRICOURT 41

trees to decorate their clothing with these green symbols of their new liberty, she, too, wore a leaf on her dress. And when the tricolour replaced this insignia she was never seen without one.

Many of Théroigne's biographers have accepted the legend that she took part in the storming of the Bastille on July 14. In 1836 a Frenchman, Lamothe-Langen, published some letters, falsely alleged to have been by her, in which her participation in the attack on the Bastille is mentioned. Since the publication of this *Correspondence de la jolie Liègeoise* romantic stories have sprung up about her gallantry on this famous fourteenth of July.

Baudelaire includes a verse about her in his sonnet *Sisina* :

> ' Avez-vous vu Théroigne, amante du carnage
> Excitant à l'assaut un peuple sans souliers,
> La joue a l'œil en feu, jouant son personnage,
> Et montant, sabre au poing, les royaux escaliers.'

Lamartine claims that ' she rushed into the street as soon as the revolt began. . . . In the front of the crowd she had forced open the iron bars to the Invalides so that the cannon could be removed. She was the first to be in the attack ; she had leapt up on to the towers of the Bastille. The conquerors had awarded her a sword of honour during the attack.' And Marcellin Pellet, who wrote about Théroigne in 1886, claims that ' she led the crowd to the Invalides . . . in search of arms.'

Théroigne herself, in her *Confessions*, says very definitely that she was ' at the Palais Royal when the Bastille was taken.' She recalls that the ' people gave way to loud and prolonged expressions of joy. Many wept for joy, crying that there would be no more Bastille, no more *lettres de cachet*.' It is clear that she is right, and that historians who attribute to her a share in the storming of the Bastille are fictionizing.

42 SEVEN WOMEN AGAINST THE WORLD

For, apart from her own statement, it was true, as Michelet later pointed out, that ' men made the fourteenth of July, just as the sixth of October was the day of the women. Men took the royal Bastille, and women took royalty itself.'

In this connection it is interesting to realize that there was one revolutionary woman, unknown except for her name—Marie Charpentier—who did join the men in their storming of the Bastille. She is included in the list of ' citoyens vanqueurs de la Bastille ' in the French National Archives ; and in the December 1789 decree of the Constituent Assembly this woman was granted a pension of two hundred livres for ' distinguishing herself in the siege of the Bastille, where she fought with the men and showed remarkable courage.'

Théroigne de Méricourt records that her active political début was on July 17, when Louis XVI returned to Paris. After the fall of the Bastille the Revolution spread everywhere. In many districts the peasants burned down manor-houses ; the prisons were opened by the rebellious crowd in Maubeuge ; revolts occurred in Lyon and Strassbourg. The old régime had virtually collapsed.

Then, as has happened in almost every revolution, liberal elements hoped to avoid the complete breakdown of the old system, to stay the tide of popular revolt. In Russia, in 1917, it was Kerensky who made this effort. In France, in 1789, such men as Bailly, the newly elected Mayor of Paris, and Lafayette, the commander of the National Guard, made a futile attempt to stop the Revolution in its course.

Louis XVI came to Paris on July 17 to ratify these new appointments. Dressed in a white riding-habit and a round hat, Théroigne marched with the soldiers of the National Guard to meet the King. She was not particularly conspicuous on this occasion, and, except for the men who had marched near her,

THÉROIGNE DE MÉRICOURT 43

no one remembered her until later when she became famous.

The National Assembly remained in Versailles, and Théroigne, who was following events as eagerly as a modern journalist, decided to move to Versailles. She rented rooms in the rue de Noailles. Soon she knew the record of each deputy; she acquired an intimate knowledge of the functioning of the Assembly. She was a regular visitor to it; a seat was reserved for her in the gallery. She was in the Assembly, and deeply moved, when feudal rights and privileges were abolished on August 4. Her Republicanism and her hatred of the aristocracy was growing stronger as she studied the situation more intelligently.

On September 23 a Regiment of Flanders was brought to Versailles, as it was feared that the people might attack, or try to abduct, the King and Marie Antoinette. The Court at Versailles committed the grave blunder of giving expression to their staunch Royalist sentiments, and the arrival of the regiment was celebrated with a banquet. This caused renewed agitation among the masses, especially in Paris, where the attitude of the Court soon became known.

Discontent was spreading rapidly in the capital; a food shortage had set in, and it was difficult to distribute such food-stuffs as were still available. This time it was the woman of Paris who began an active revolt. A woman, whose name is unknown, organized a mass meeting at the Café de Foy; another beat a drum in the *Halles*, calling upon the women of Paris to march to Versailles to fetch the King and the Queen.

According to legend, Théroigne is said to have had a great deal to do with this march to Versailles by the women. Actually, of course, this is pure invention, as she was already living in Versailles. In her own account of the day, she denies that she was in Paris, and that she marched with the women to

44 SEVEN WOMEN AGAINST THE WORLD

Versailles. This has not prevented many historians from describing her gallant actions on this day. More than that, some writers have given a most fantastic description of her on this occasion.

De Goncourt has really let himself go : ' To horse, when the hour of October struck,' he wrote, ' with red plumes, riding habit of red silk, this radiant Penthesilea, this Amazon of Rubens, riding-whip in hand, revolvers in her belt, galloped in her triumph, in front of the crowd, smiling, with sleeves rolled up to the elbow. It is the beautiful woman of Liège, bringing to Versailles pikes which are asking for heads, and women who are demanding the destruction of the Queen.'

As a matter of fact, of course, as has been said, Théroigne was in Versailles when the weary procession of women arrived from Paris. It is true, however, that, though she did not act as an Amazon on this occasion, she now frequently wore men's clothes. She herself wrote that she had a red and a white riding-habit, and Michelet described her on this sixth of October as ' . . . a native of Liège, lively and passionate . . . interesting, original, and odd with her riding-habit and hat, a sword at her side, speaking a mixture of French and the Liège patois, yet eloquent.'

The exhausted women from Paris were a depressing and moving sight. Jean-Joseph Mounier, the president of the National Assembly, who officially received them in Versailles, has left a description of them. ' The women crowded round me,' Mounier writes, ' declaring that they wanted to accompany me to the King's palace. I had great difficulty in making them understand that only six of them would be able to see the King, but that did not prevent many of them from swelling the procession.

' We were on foot, in the mud ; a heavy rain was falling. A large crowd of Versailles inhabitants lined

THÉROIGNE DE MÉRICOURT 45

both sides of the avenue which led to the palace. The women of Paris had come in various groups. With them were a few men, most of them dressed in rags. Their appearance was fierce and their gestures were menacing. They were armed with muskets, old pikes, hatchets, iron bars, and large poles.'

Théroigne had spent the afternoon at the meeting of the National Assembly. She came out at five o'clock and saw the crowd of tired women standing in the rain. She went from group to group trying to encourage them. Then, so she writes in her *Confessions*, she left the women, and a friend took her home.

' I went to the corner of the road in which I lived,' she remembered, ' where my friend left me. I forced my way through as far as the barrier. There I saw on the one hand the Regiment of Flanders, and on the other the Bodyguard of the people armed with guns. Pushing my way along I met three or four unfortunate creatures [among the soldiers] who were weeping. They told me that they had not had a mouthful of bread for three days. I took them with me near to where I lodged, got some bread from my rooms, and divided it among them.'

This slight act of kindness was to have disastrous results for Théroigne. She was later accused of having given the soldiers not bread but money, as a bribe to prevent them from shooting into the crowd of women if this became necessary to protect the King and Queen.

It is odd that this unjust accusation should have been held against her when, actually, in this, one of her great moments, she went further than merely giving the soldiers money : she urged them under no circumstances to shoot at the helpless women. Her sincerity, her plea, and the obvious solidarity she felt for all those who were oppressed were far more effective—and more dangerous to the discipline of the army—than a few coins could possibly have been.

46 SEVEN WOMEN AGAINST THE WORLD

Her dignity on this occasion must have been superb, and Carlyle's description of the scene is grotesque.

' But already Pallas Athene (in the shape of Mademoiselle Théroigne) ', he writes, ' is busy with Flanders and the dismounted dragoons. She, and such women as are fittest, go through the ranks, speak with an earnest jocosity, clasp rough troopers to their patriot bosoms, crush down spontoons and musketoons with soft arms : can a man that were worthy of the name of man, attack famishing patriot women ? '

After she had calmed the soldiers, Théroigne went home and remained there until early the next morning, when she went to the National Assembly. She is quite positive that ' she did not leave her rooms again that night, although she knew that the deputies had been convoked for a special all-night session.'

This statement is most important, for she was also accused later of having joined or even having led the outraged women, who at five o'clock that morning rushed into the palace shouting, ' To the Queen's apartments ! ' Marie Antoinette was saved at the last moment by escaping to the King's rooms. The furious women were already beating down the door to her bedroom, and, as Stefan Zweig very wisely says : ' The family was reunited, their lives had been saved, but nothing more than their lives.'

One of the reasons why Théroigne's enemies were convinced that she had been involved in the plot to murder Marie Antoinette was that she never failed to express her hatred of the aristocracy in vehement terms. Discussing the events of the night with her friends, or with strangers, the next day, she undoubtedly condoned the action of the women who had stormed the palace. Théroigne never learned to remain silent in a crisis.

The morning of October 7 Théroigne left her rooms in the rue de Noailles at about six o'clock and returned to the National Assembly. The doors had not yet been opened, and a huge crowd stood round the building.

'I moved amongst this crowd of people,' Théroigne writes, 'for I wanted to hear what they were saying. They were discussing the aristocrats, and I joined in and spoke no good of them. Then I tried to glide in amongst the ranks of the National Guard; my attention was attracted by the clamouring of the people who were fighting with the Bodyguard. But I could not see distinctly what was going on.

'At last the doors to the Assembly were opened. I went to my usual seat in Tribune Number VI. The hall was almost empty, only a few of the deputies of the aristocracy were present. Under the circumstances they demanded that the National Assembly should be moved to the Hercules Gallery in the palace. It seemed to me and to all those present in the gallery that a removal of the representatives would violate the decrees of the National Assembly. We made strenuous opposition to this. We all thought it would be better if a numerous deputation was sent to the King. This was agreed upon.'

The fact that during these momentous days Théroigne preferred the gallery in the National Assembly to the crowded streets is significant of her restrained frame of mind at this particular period. Later she became the Amazon she is generally considered, but at this stage of the Revolution it was her ambition to become a politician. She wanted to further the Republican cause by political means rather than by street-fighting. She took an intellectual rather than a belligerent part in it.

Her old friends were struck by the change in her when she returned to Paris in the autumn of 1789. For when the National Assembly was moved there from Versailles she followed. She wore simple clothes, and her serious interests were reflected in her

48 SEVEN WOMEN AGAINST THE WORLD

sober demeanour. As one of her contemporaries said, ' The voluptuous gypsy had been metamorphosed into a grave and severe Minerva.'

In Paris she was no longer satisfied with casual political discussions, with indiscriminate enthusiasm. The influence of the great and influential political clubs was at its height ; many of them were being organized as imitations of the Jacobin Club or the Cordelier Club, of which Danton, Marat, and Desmoulins were members. Later, in 1791, the Legislative Assembly made a vain effort to limit the growing power of these clubs, but they were then too firmly established in France.

Théroigne received many politicians in her modest rooms at the Hôtel de Grenoble in the rue Bouloi. It annoyed her profoundly when her social activities were called a ' salon.' Already she was developing keen feminist instincts, and she hated this term which was applied to the political gatherings arranged by women.

She therefore founded a political club known as the *Amis de la Loi.* Her chief associate and the official president of the club—she could not avoid making this concession to the prestige of men—was Gilbert Romme, a member of the National Assembly. He helped to devise the Republican calendar. In 1793 he committed suicide by stabbing himself, because he wanted ' to cheat the guillotine.'

At Théroigne's club the problems of the day were feverishly discussed, but these debates were of academic importance only. Her theoretical phase as a revolutionary had no influence, for it did not really matter whether or not such visitors to it as Mirabeau, Broglie, or de Liancourt, sat talking with her at her club or not. Besides, the questions Théroigne suggested for discussion, the resolutions she passed, were entirely theoretical. She wanted, for instance, ' to give new impulse to manners,' to 'educate the people to an understanding of the dignity of their rights,' to 'display before the people the advantages of the Revolution,' and to 'awaken patriotism which was extinct among some.'

At this time, as these resolutions show, she was far removed from that violence which during a later period of her life she firmly believed to be necessary in the Revolution. While she was the leading spirit in her club she expressively hoped, as its name, *Les Amis de la Loi* indicated, that the upheaval in France would be achieved by peaceful means. In fact one of the statutes of the club emphasized this point of view : it was to be one of the functions of *Les Amis de la Loi* to 'restrain some of the too excitable spirits who might be carried away by their excess of zeal.'

Théroigne was already a supporter of the feminist movement, as an ardent defender of which she afterwards called the women of Paris to arms. She was enthusiastic about the *Société Fraternelle des Patriots des deux Sexes*, and her loyalty towards her own sex was an unusual characteristic in a woman whose early life had been spent so exclusively with men. She was in close touch with the militant feminists of the French Revolution : Etta Palm, Rose Lacombe, and Rose Renaut ; and she firmly believed, as Olympe de George said, that if women had the right in the Revolution to mount the scaffold, they should also have the right to mount the Tribunal.

'*Citoyennes*,' Théroigne once asked her fellow-countrywomen, 'why do we not enter into rivalry with men ? They pretend that they alone have the right to achieve glory. No, indeed, this should not be. We also wish to merit a civic crown, to compete for the honour of dying for the liberty which is perhaps dearer to us than to them, because the effects of despotism weigh more heavily upon us than upon them.'

4

50 SEVEN WOMEN AGAINST THE WORLD

It was Théroigne's tragedy that neither her feminism nor her Republicanism were strong enough to make her persevere in any movement. She was too unstable to go on when she confronted failure ; she could not bear the disapproval of others, and ridicule crushed her entirely. She was ill for days when one Royalist newspaper called her a ' a heroine of the boudoir.'

Théroigne never developed that uncomprising fanaticism which has caused other women revolutionaries to forget everything but their Cause. If Théroigne was in debt, or a slighting verse had appeared about her in a Royalist newspaper, or one of her beloved brothers was not well, she became a worried woman. Until this anxiety passed she was no longer a revolutionary. And intermittent fanaticism is not fanaticism at all; it cannot achieve results.

She was miserable when her club failed. She had worked herself up into a state of expectancy, hoping that she would be able to persuade the new Government to move the National Assembly into a more fitting building. When she laid the plans for this venture before numerous representatives and they did not take them seriously, she was in despair.

She was in this depressed mood when, in August 1790, the Châtelet Court issued a warrant for her arrest. She was accused of having taken part in the attempt on the Queen's life on the night of October 6. She was badly frightened when she heard of this, and she became panicky when she was informed by friends that the Tribunal was prejudiced against her.

She herself wrote later that she had been ' astonished at this news, but that she remained quite calm, as she believed herself to be entirely innocent,' but she admits that she ' realized that if the accusation was serious she would have to defend herself.' Actually, however, she did not remain calm nor did she stay in

THÉROIGNE DE MÉRICOURT 51

Paris to defend herself. Her return to Liège was more like a flight than a visit to her brothers.

Even her fear, however, had not made Théroigne cautious. Perhaps she had never acquired self-control, perhaps she was courageous when actually confronted with an enemy. At any rate, during the entire diligence journey to Liège she not only announced her Republican principles to any one who would listen to her; she was as rude as possible to the 'coarse aristocrats' who travelled with her. She became insulting when they spoke of the masses of the people as the 'lower orders,' and at an inn, where she stayed the night, she forgot her resolution to pretend that she was quite unpolitical, and made an impassioned speech against despotism in general and the French Royalists in particular.

As one of her listeners was an Austrian officer, and as they were very near the frontier of the Austrian Netherlands by this time, her outburst was extremely rash. Besides, she was advertising her presence, which was soon reported to Count Mercy-Argenteau, who was then the Austrian Ambassador to the Low Countries.

Count Mercy had been sent to Paris as Maria Theresa's representative when Marie Antoinette went there as a very young and inexperienced girl, and he was devoted to the Queen. Mercy was, of course, particularly antagonistic towards Théroigne, who, so he was sure, had been in some way responsible for the attempt on the Queen's life. Besides, he had been informed of the Chatelet Court's accusation against her.

Théroigne returned to Marcourt, her native village, quite unaware that her indiscretion on the journey might have disastrous consequences. 'I cannot express the pleasure I felt when I arrived,' she writes, ' or my joy at seeing my village again, the house where I was born, my uncle, and the comrades of my

52 SEVEN WOMEN AGAINST THE WORLD

youth. I quite forgot about the French Revolution. Every evening I went to the *veillée*, and with my friends I joined in all the games of our youth. On Sundays we went to dance, to run and play in the open fields.'

Théroigne is probably quite truthful when she says that she 'forgot the French Revolution,' but it is obvious that she did not forget it for more than a few hours at a time. She did not spend her entire holiday playing innocent games with the villagers. Instead, she talked to them with enthusiasm about the Revolution ; she taught them the revolutionary songs which were popular in Paris ; she enlightened them about the aristocrats with whom she had come into contact. In other words, she spread revolutionary propaganda both in Marcourt and in Tilleur, another village near Liège, where she went later.

All sorts of rumours were soon spread about her. Emperor Leopold II, who had succeeded his brother Joseph II in February 1790, was naturally trying to overcome the revolutionary feeling which had sprung up in his dominions after the French Revolution. Spying was in the air. Some people thought that Théroigne was an Austrian agent ; others that she had come from France to incite the people in the Low Countries to revolution. This opinion was confirmed by many French Royalist refugees, who hated her quite as much as she hated them. The wildest tales were told about her in the district. Then, as now, simple people were irresistibly attracted to any one who might be a spy, no matter for what government or for what cause. Théroigne had created a stir, not so much because of the Republican principles she had preached, but for the less glorious reason that she was a talkative woman.

Count Kaunitz, Leopold II's Foreign Minister, was less concerned with her propagandist activities than with the fact that, as he believed, she had incited

THÉROIGNE DE MÉRICOURT 53

the crowd to murder Marie Antoinette, his sovereign's
sister. The night of October 6, 1789, when Théroigne
slept peacefully in her bed, had become the most
important date in her life.

Count Mercy-Argenteau sent a message to Kaunitz
advising him to curb Théroigne in some way or other.
Finally Mercy's messages became more urgent. ' . . .
I am also told about the woman called Théroigne de
Méricourt,' he reported to the Foreign Minister,
'who was at the head of the Queen's enemies on
October the fifth and the sixth. She is to be found in
the province of Luxemburg, and carries on a correspondence with our *enragés* in Paris and Liège. A
Frenchmen with good letters of recommendation
came to ask my permission to kidnap her and her
papers secretly. I have sanctioned this act, and
ordered his escort to be strengthened by a small
mounted patrol. If the capture is made they will
conduct the prisoner to Freiburg, there to await whatever fate may be decided upon as most suitable for
her.'

In the night from the fifteenth to the sixteenth of
February 1791, a Frenchman, named de la Valette,
broke into Théroigne's rooms with an escort, and she
was carried by force to a diligence. She herself had
no idea why she was being kidnapped. De la Valette
was accompanied by another French officer, both of
them Royalists, and by an Austrian officer. She
demanded to see the order for her arrest, but naturally,
as the Austrian Government merely approved of this
act and did not want to be officially connected with
it, the officers had no order for her detention.

Théroigne was first taken to Coblentz and then to
Worms, where among others the old Prince de Condé,
now the head of the Royalist *émigrés*, wanted to see
her. She turned her back on him haughtily. From
Worms she was taken to Freiburg in Breisgau, then
to Innsbruck, from where she was finally brought to

54 SEVEN WOMEN AGAINST THE WORLD

the Fortress Prison in Kufstein, where she was locked up in a cell.

Even on this journey she talked to her military escorts about the Revolution. She almost converted one of them, a Baron de Landresc, who travelled with her to Innsbruck. She was very gentle with him, she did not shout at him. She merely told him that ' it should be the aim of every well-born human being to help the unfortunate and the oppressed,' and that ' in this great work there need be no discrimination between men and women.'

In the Kufstein Fortress it became obvious that Théroigne was a better propagandist than she was an active revolutionary. For, to put it bluntly, she broke down completely. Her later madness had already cast a shadow upon her, for she screamed hysterically when she was put into her cell; her unstable nervous system made it unbearable for her to be shut up in a confining space. Her warders were startled, for they had heard and believed that she was indeed an ' Amazon.'

The possessions she brought to Kufstein should have warned the prison authorities that Théroigne was in an extremely feminine mood. She had packed no riding-habits or revolvers when she was so suddenly told to leave her rooms in Tilleur. The list of her things still exists : one hat, two frocks, one silk scarf, one brown coat trimmed with fur, one muff, two pairs of shoes, four undergarments, five handkerchiefs, ten pairs of silk stockings, one belt, Plato's *Dialogues*, and a volume of the works of Seneca.

At Kufstein she was allowed to read, she had plenty of food, and she was well treated. She was moved into a cell with two windows in it, and she was often permitted to walk in the prison courtyard. Le Blanc, the Governor of the prison, was particularly attentive to her; her nervous state had not affected the charm she exercised on men.

THÉROIGNE DE MÉRICOURT 55

At times, while she waited in Kufstein for six months for her trial, she was calmer. Then she would forget for a moment where she was, and be worried by relatively trivial troubles. ' Perhaps you have been obliged to sell my piano,' she wrote to her brother Pierre on July 29, ' in spite of the fact that it cost me thirty louis. This would make me sad, and I shall never be able to afford another. But after all it is but a small misfortune. . . . Have you looked after my belongings at the Bovarie ? I am afraid that my dresses will be spoilt, especially the woollen ones, if you have not had them put out to air. Above all, I recommend my books to your care. Do not lend them to any one. Use them only for your own instruction and for our brother.'

As the weeks passed her more normal moods grew less frequent. Théroigne was in a constant state of morbid depression. De Blanc became seriously alarmed about her. Dr. de Mederer, a physician famous in Austria at the time, was called in to examine her. He found her in good physical condition, but he was afraid that the mental strain was too much for her. He was interested in her case, and urged the prison authorities to give her every possible consideration.

' How many people gifted with these extraordinary powers,' Dr. de Mederer wrote in his diagnosis of Théroigne, ' if they employ them continually on one idea, as occurred and still occurs in the case of this highly strung prisoner, are liable to weaken and destroy both body and mind so completely as to have great difficulty in restoring them. This is an acknowledged fact, which is so generally known that it is hardly necessary to furnish proof of it.'

De Mederer's diagnosis was sent to Kaunitz, who asked Leopold II to have Théroigne brought to Vienna at once. The Austrian Government was beginning to feel somewhat uncomfortable about her arrest.

56 SEVEN WOMEN AGAINST THE WORLD

When she reached Vienna, therefore, Théroigne was not sent to prison. She lived in a private house with a maid. She was carefully watched by the police, but she was allowed to move about freely.

This condition of semi-liberty irked Théroigne almost as much as the prison had depressed her. She was now willing to promise anything if she could be released and leave Austria. She promised that she would go and live in any place suggested by the Austrian Government. Nothing, however, was decided before her trial, which was arranged for November 24.

It is interesting that she was tried as 'Madame Lahaye,' for the Austrian Government was determined to avoid unpleasant publicity. Her behaviour at her trial was surprising. From a weary and broken woman she changed suddenly into an aggressive defender of democratic principles. As soon as she had an attentive audience, and knew that her future freedom was at stake, she pulled herself together and shouted fearlessly at the judge. No one could ever foretell what Théroigne de Méricourt would do next; whether she would not change from a weeping woman into a fighting Amazon in a few moments. For this reason she frightened some men as much as she attracted them.

The judge was furious: 'It is not enough,' he reprimanded her, 'that we should have to read columns of lamentable details concerning the incidents of the French Revolution in the reports of your verbal hearings and other documents regarding your case. But you seem to consider it necessary to add your personal opinions in regard to the causes of this catastrophe. Not content with describing terrible and bloodthirsty scenes in poetical language, you do not hesitate—madly eager to proselyte as you are—to try to persuade us that the reasons you give for your revolutionary frenzy are excellent ones. . . . It is

THÉROIGNE DE MÉRICOURT   57

your democratic fanaticism, and that of others like you, which is at the root of the evil. This is culpable, and it is the cause of the present impossible state of affairs in France. Is his Majesty Louis XVI responsible for the troubles and scandals of Paris and Versailles ? No, he is not. It is the mad folly of such as you. Without the devilish passion which possesses you and blinds you and your co-religionists in Paris, there would be no cries of upheaval, no struggles, no tears, and no blood in the streets of the capital.'

After this bitter attack from the judge, Théroigne must have realized that her position was most precarious. But now, though she knew what effect prison life had on her, she defended her ideas. She had again changed : this time into a really heroic woman. Regardless of the tortures which a new term of imprisonment would mean to her, he did not let the judge intimidate her. She said :

' My ideas are what they are, and it is useless for you to use such eloquent words and gestures to contradict me. The truth is that I am a fervent patriot and a good citizen. You condemn the Republic; that is your duty. I, on the other hand, condemn the Monarchy, and I think I am right in doing so. Besides, I have only one hope. This is that the principles of '89 and the acknowledgement of the Rights of Men will prevail throughout Europe and in every country in the world. In this work I have tried to help.'

Perhaps the Court was impressed by her courage, perhaps the Austrian Government had planned to release her in any case. Whatever the cause, she was told to go after the trial, because she was free. She returned to Paris in January 1792, where she was welcomed as a heroine.

For her return to the capital Théroigne discarded her feminine weakness and her feminine clothes. She

58 SEVEN WOMEN AGAINST THE WORLD

appeared in the Jacobin Club wearing a soldier's coat, and a hat with a huge plume in it. She absorbed the more radical atmosphere which now prevailed in France. She approved of the new Legislative Assembly which had succeeded the National Assembly in October 1791. She now heard first-hand accounts of the King and Queen's unsuccessful flights to Varennes in June of that year. She was aware that the Revolution was again at a critical stage. She was a Moderate no longer, though later she was again troubled by doubts about the efficacy of violent methods. She considered those of her fellow-countrymen who were still opposed to maintaining the Revolution by force if necessary as counter-revolutionaries. She herself was ready and prepared to fight on the barricades.

She believed, furthermore, that all healthy women should fight with men ; she had become a passionate feminist. Her career as an Amazon had begun in earnest. ' Legislators,' she had appealed to the Legislative Assembly, ' women patriots present themselves to you to claim their individual right to defend their lives and their liberty.'

Most of her male contemporaries were furious when she called upon the women. These men wanted to revolutionize society, but they did not welcome any change in their own family life. They were willing and eager to fight in the streets all day, but they wanted their wives and a good meal to be awaiting them when they came home. Even the members of the revolutionary *Société des Defenseurs des Droits de l'homme et des ennemis du Despotism*—on April 13—complained about her to Robespierre.

Despite these attacks Théroigne continued to devote herself to recruiting those women revolutionaries who were willing to fight in the ranks, for it was clear that the crisis was approaching. ' To arms, to arms ! ' she began many street corner meetings each

THÉROIGNE DE MÉRICOURT 59

day, ' let us show men that we are not inferior to them either in virtue or in courage.'

It is not known in what part of Paris Théroigne was speaking on the twentieth of June when the population revolted against the Monarchy, but her activities on the tenth of August, when the King was deposed, are well documented. Her actions in the riots which broke out on that day are connected in history with the death of a Royalist named Suleau, who had attacked her some years before in his newspaper *Les Actes des Apôtres.*

During the Revolution Suleau had gone to Coblentz, where he had taken an active part in the intrigues of the Royalist refugees. In 1792 he returned to France ; in the disguise of a National Guardsman, he was trying to win support for the Royalist cause and studying the ' temper of the people.'

On the tenth of August, when the fury of the population against the Royalists was at its height, Théroigne de Méricourt was standing in the Place Vendôme on an improvised platform addressing a crowd. She did not know Suleau personally, but some one pointed him out to her as he passed. It has never been known whether she actually killed him herself, or whether, as a contemporary claims, she ' designated him to a hired assassin standing near her, who thereupon massacred him and dragged his body to the right-hand corner of the Place Vendôme.'

Violence is always terrible, and the only excuse for it is the revolutionaries' conviction that, as history has so often proven, it is at times inevitable. Soldiers in the Great War could not be pictured as gallant heroes, if the countries ringing their praises did not believe that they were fighting for some gallant or just cause. Unless a war, either international or civil, is thought to be a ' holy war,' violence is murder.

Most revolutionary women who have committed acts of violence are, of course, as heroic, or more so,

60 SEVEN WOMEN AGAINST THE WORLD

than any soldier : these women have believed in the sacredness of their cause. Théroigne's act is robbed of its heroic qualities, because she was prompted to kill Suleau as much by a desire for personal revenge as she was by the fact that he was a Royalist and therefore an enemy.

Even in her violent mood, however, she remained attractive. Baron Thiebault, a Lieutenant-General in the French Army, who witnessed this scene, admitted ' with a shudder ' that she was very handsome, and made more beautiful still by her excitement. ' Preceded by a group of maniacs,' he continues his description of Suleau's death, ' she pushed her way through the crowd and leapt up on to a cannon.'

The death of Suleau, and Théroigne's bravery in the streets on the tenth of August, won for her the highest praise of the revolutionary government. The *Moniteur* for September 3 announced that Mesdemoiselles Théroigne, Lacombe, and Reine Andu were awarded civic crowns for their distinguished courage on August the tenth.

Some of Théroigne's biographers, who consistently associate her name with the Girondists, claim that she broke off all relations with the extremists immediately after the August uprising. These biographers are obviously repelled by the thought that their heroine persisted in associating with men who believed in and practised violence after she had actually witnessed street-fighting and bloodshed. They are undoubtedly wrong, however, for as reliable a writer as Dr. John Moore, who was at the time a member of the household of the British Ambassador in Paris, saw her at the Jacobin Club on August 17. More than that, she was not in the club merely as a guest and an observer, but as an active participant in the deliberations of the members. Dr. Moore writes :

' There were abundance of women in the galleries, but as there were none in the body of the hall where the members were seated, I was surprised to see one enter and take her seat amongst them. She was dressed in a kind of English riding-habit, but her jacket was the uniform of the National Guards. On inquiry I was informed that the name of this Amazon is Mademoiselle Théroigne; she distinguished herself in the action of the tenth by rallying those who fled, and attacking a second time at the head of the Marseillais. She seems about one-and-thirty, is somewhat above the middle size of women, and has a smart martial air, which in a man would be disagreeable.'

Apart from John Moore's statement, there is no record of Théroigne's activities during the eventful winter of 1792-93. The Girondists were temporarily in power. When, in September, the Legislative Assembly was followed by the Convention, the moderate Girondists, now the conservers in the literal sense of the word, retained a strong position against the Montagnards, then including such men as Robespierre, Marat, Danton, and the Duc d'Orleans, ' Philippe Egalité.'

Any definite facts concerning Théroigne's attitude or actions during the September massacres would be of the greatest interest. One thing is certain—judging by her mental state after she went mad—and that is that she experienced a terrible conflict. Throughout her efforts to militarize the women of Paris she had called on them to arm, to use violence, if necessary, to defend their rights. In September, when she saw the effects of the terror, her nerves must have given way. And yet she could not bring herself to abandon the ideas of the Jacobins entirely; she still lived at 273 rue Saint Honore, near the Jacobin Club, so that she often met the members in the street and talked to them.

She suffered the tormenting indecision which modern Socialists must go through when they make their choice between Communism and the pacifist

62 SEVEN WOMEN AGAINST THE WORLD

doctrines of Social Democracy. She was aware that there was little time to lose, just as to-day the enemies of Fascism cannot wait indefinitely. Théroigne realized that both the Moderates and the Extremists in the French Revolution were in imminent danger from the same enemy.

In the end Théroigne moved more to the Right ; her horror of the violence overcame her prejudices against the Girondists. She escaped from the doubts which still tormented her into a hope that the Moderates and Montagnards would unite. An appeal she made early in May—it was printed by Dufart, a printer in the rue Saint Honoré—was an impassioned plea for a ' United Front,' as we call this co-operation of left-wing parties in our own day.

She was fully aware that the Republic was, as she expressed it, ' almost on the edge of the precipice.' France was at war with almost all of Europe, and after the French defeat at Neerwinden in March, and the flight of Dumouriez, the Girondist general, there was a grave danger that France might be invaded by the enemy. If the Austrian, British, and Prussian armies had been more firmly united they could have marched on to Paris. Then, as Théroigne knew, the Monarchy would be restored. In the end, only the uncomprising and ruthless attitude of the Committee of Public Safety, which was organized in July, prevented this calamity.

These months of waiting were unforgettable to French Republicans. So profound was the impression left by the fear that the Monarchy might be restored with the help of foreign invaders, that in 1871, when the Commune was established, this fear of 1793 still influenced the attitude of the French people.

In her appeal, Théroigne pointed out the dangers of the situation, and urged all Republicans to unite. ' I am not going to utter fine phrases,' she said, ' I am going to tell you the pure and simple truth. Where

THÉROIGNE DE MÉRICOURT 63

do we stand ? The many conflicting passions which have been roused may carry us away. . . . Citizens, let us stop and reflect . . . it is one of the calumnies of Kings and their slaves to pretend that it is not possible for the people to assemble and to exercise their sovereignty without abusing it. This is a part of the great conspiracy against democracy.'

Then she warned the people : ' Even united we are none too strong to repulse our numerous enemies from without, and those who have already raised the standard of rebellion. Nevertheless I warn you that our enemies will make no distinction between the parties ; we shall all be confounded on the day of vengeance. . . . Danger must reunite us, and we are going to show you what men who desire liberty and who work for the cause of the human race can do.'

Théroigne now worked incessantly for the United Front, trying to point out to both the Moderates and the Extremists that they must be more tolerant of each other. She had not learned that during a crisis any one trying to see both sides of a political question is usually considered a traitor by both. That was her tragedy, and it was to be her destruction as well.

On the fifteenth of May she met a group of excited women near the Place Vendôme. One of them at once attacked Théroigne for being friendly with Brissot, who had been expelled from the Jacobin Club the autumn before for his moderate views. Théroigne defended him. She tried to calm the women, speaking to them as she had spoken to thousands of Paris women before. They would not listen to her. Instead, they undressed her and beat her ferociously. They would have killed her if Marat had not happened to come upon this terrible scene. He drove the women off and saved Théroigne's life.

' A heroine of the revolution experienced a rebuff the day before yesterday,' the *Courrier des Départements* wrote somewhat calmly. ' On the seventeenth

64 SEVEN WOMEN AGAINST THE WORLD

of May, Mademoiselle Théroigne, who, it is alleged, was recruiting women for the faction of Monsieur Roland, unfortunately addressed herself to the followers of Robespierre and Marat. These women, not wishing to increase the Brissotin army, seized the female recruiter and beat her with great activity. The Guard arrived and saved the victim from the fury of these indecent maniacs. Marat, who was passing, took the beaten woman under his protection.'

Lamartine, de Goncourt, and others say that Théroigne went mad immediately after the shock of this terrible experience, but Frank Hamel, who published a biography of her in 1911, points out that George Forster, the Rector of the University of Mayence, who was representing that city in Paris, saw her two months later, when she seemed quite normal. Besides, on July 5, she wrote a calm business letter to her bankers, Messieurs le Contenaux et Companie, and she appeared to be no more nervous than usual about her financial affairs.

In the spring of 1794, however, her brother Joseph, whom she had sent to Rome to study painting, and who now lived in Paris, was seriously alarmed about her. He published a notice saying that his sister was no longer in a fit mental condition to enter into any business arrangements. For her own safety he urged that she be put under restraint. Later, when he was afraid that she might be guillotined, he offered to take the full responsibility for her care, and asked that she be allowed to live in his home. This request was not granted.

On September 20, 1794, her madness was certified. When she was first taken to an asylum in the Faubourg-Marceau her troubled brain was haunted by the terrible belief that she was under arrest. ' I am still under arrest,' she wrote to Saint-Just two days before his death ; ' I have written to you to beg you to send me two hundred livres and to come to see me. They

THÉROIGNE DE MÉRICOURT 65

ought not to be indifferent to the fact that I am here and that I am doing nothing.'

She lived on for twenty-three years in various asylums. Her physical health was good. In her madness she could not bear to wear any clothes ; water had an abnormal attraction for her, and she would pour buckets of it on her bed, on the floor. She spoke only to ' revile everybody, speaking only of liberty, of committees, of public safety, of revolutionary organizations.'

The conflict she experienced during the September massacres obviously tormented her to the end. Always she was dimly haunted by the thought that she should have had the courage of her convictions, even if they made violence inevitable : for seventeen years she cried out in her madness against the Moderates.

III

FLORA TRISTAN (1803–1844)

WHEN, in 1843, Flora Tristan published her *L'Union Ouvrière*, in which she urged the workers of France to unite, the meaning of the word ' revolutionary ' was rapidly changing. Karl Marx's *Communist Manifesto*, published four years later, in 1847, and the insurrections which swept through Europe in 1848, made it quite clear that this word had, in fact, been given an entirely new interpretation.

The French Revolution had been the classic struggle between the ' people ' and the privileged classes of the aristocracy. Now the people themselves were becoming conscious of the unsurmountable differences which separated them into two distinct and antagonistic classes. The word ' Socialist ' was first used in 1827, in the *Co-operative Magazine*.

The workers' uprising in Paris, the ' glorious three days ' in July 1830, caused the propertied bourgeoisie to realize without a doubt that it would have to defend its economic supremacy, if necessary, by force. The working classes, on the other hand, the proletariat as they were called, were awakening to a growing appreciation of their rights as human beings, and they, too, were slowly preparing to fight for these rights.

Many sincere humanitarians, in England as well as in France, were devoting their lives to improving conditions among the industrial wage earners. Reform was in the air, and men like Robert Owen, in England, or François Fourier, in France, were making an effort to enlighten the more wealthy and privileged classes to a realization of their responsibilities towards the

68 SEVEN WOMEN AGAINST THE WORLD

poor and the oppressed. These ardent reformers were preaching with unflagging courage that those in power must make a drastic change in the structure of society, that the rights of working men and women must be recognized in any country calling itself civilized.

Flora Tristan's greatness lies in her early realization that reform of this kind was not enough. Advocates of a reorganization of society were writing about the working classes, they were pleading their cause. Flora Tristan, on the other hand, went just that step beyond these reformers, which in the end became the basis for later revolutionary movements. She did not foresee that Marx and his followers would be urging the proletariat to prepare for the class war, to fight for their rights, but she did realize that the workers would not be materially helped by outside agencies, no matter how humanitarian they might be, or by the activities of men who did not themselves belong to the working classes.

She said : No, society as a whole cannot help the workers. Kind individuals among the upper classes cannot really change their lot by reform. No one can realize this improvement but the workers themselves. With this firm belief in mind, Flora Tristan, in contrast to other reformers of her day, addressed her *Union Ouvrière* to the workers themselves, telling them that only through their own joint efforts could they accomplish anything.

In view of her outstanding contribution to the development of thought in France, it is strange that she has been practically forgotten by historians and by students of social history. The leaves of the earlier edition of her book were found uncut in the British Museum—more than ninety years after it was published —and she is ignored in most books about distinguished women. To-day, unjust as this is, her claim to distinction is confined almost exclusively to the fame of her grandson, Paul Gauguin. But even some of his biographies do not do her justice. In Jean de Roton-champ's biography of Gauguin, for instance, she is referred to merely as ' a woman who at the time enjoyed a certain notoriety.'

Perhaps if Flora Tristan's death had been as dramatic as her life, she would have been more generally remembered. But the premature death of so many women is caused directly or indirectly by overwork, by their fanatical devotion to their duty as they see it, and history easily overlooks their daily sacrifice. Their tireless efforts are often overshadowed by one spectacular sacrifice made by other and less able women.

Everything about Flora Tristan—her parentage, her childhood, her marriage, her character, her whole life —is restless, uncertain, and highly strung. She herself and nothing about her ever relaxed into a peaceful state of everyday existence. Her parents, products of their age, never sat back quietly to contemplate and, much less, to enjoy life, and Flora seemed to rush through her relatively short career. Rarely did she have a permanent address.

Her mother, Thérèse Lainé, who experienced a disturbed childhood during the French Revolution, had fled to Spain with an elderly relative. In Bilbao these two women lived as uprooted refugees. Flora's father, Don Mariano de Tristan, who came of an old Peruvian family, was restless by temperament as well as by circumstances. A born adventurer, he was a Colonel in the Spanish Army when he met Thérèse Lainé and fell in love with her.

Don Mariano wanted to marry her, and it would have been quite simple for a man of his standing to obtain the King of Spain's permission for a civil marriage. This consent for officers serving in the Spanish Army was only a matter of form. For some unknown reason, however, Don Mariano never made this slight effort, though he was devoted to Thérèse

70 SEVEN WOMEN AGAINST THE WORLD

until his death six years later. What prevented him from bothering about a legal marriage was probably a temperamental aversion to being bound to anything or to any one. He never left Thérèse, but he felt that, legally, he could do so at any moment. This peculiar attitude did not harm his family as long as he lived, but it made their financial position disastrous after his death, for Thérèse, not being an official widow, could not inherit his fortune.

Thérèse had at first objected to these informal arrangements, but as she ' could not live without him,' she finally agreed, and they were married in her rooming house by a French *émigré* priest, who had no legal right whatsoever to perform this ceremony. This was in 1802.

Late that year, some months before Flora was born, Thérèse returned to France with her elderly relative. Don Mariano soon followed, and Flora—Flore-Cêlèste-Thérèse Tristan—was born on April 7, 1803. The vague recollections Flora retained of her house and garden near Paris were her only peaceful memories. Actually, Don Mariano's life was anything but secure and orderly, for though he had a considerable income, he could never be sure whether or not his allowance would arrive safely from Peru. Large portions of his fortune were confiscated by the British ; other sums went down with the vessel *Minerva*. Don Mariano need never have feared that his existence would become too settled, secure, or dull.

At this time he seems to have found an outlet for his adventurous spirit by long and excited conversations with his old friend Simon Bolivar, *the Liberator* of South America. Don Mariano derived tremendous vicarious satisfaction from Bolivar's heated controversies with the Bonapartists, by whom he was attacked as a ' Jacobin.' Flora first heard such terms as ' human liberty ' and ' oppression ' from Bolivar and her father, who tried to explain to her what the

FLORA TRISTAN

South American meant when he replied to the Bona-partists by saying that ' the blood-thirsty name of Jacobins is given by them to all lovers of liberty who oppose Napoleon or called his followers Royalists.'

Flora would have continued to pick up scraps of useful information from her father. He was too dis-organized himself to have given her a systematic training, but at least she would have begun her career with some sort of knowledge. As it was, he died in 1807 or 1808, leaving Thérèse penniless, and not even a widow in the eyes of the Law. She moved to the country with her two children, and wrote twenty letters to Don Mariano's relatives in Peru asking them to help her.

Thérèse did any work she could find, spending her emotional energy in waiting for the answers to these letters which never came. She had no time to teach Flora anything. Thérèse's bitter resentment to her terrible poverty made her emphasize in the girl's mind the injustice of a fate which had made them poor, while, by right of birth, by privilege of the great Peruvian family from which she came, she would have been rich and influential.

Flora was fast developing a prima donna attitude towards life. In fact, during her early girlhood, she was a snob, who looked down upon the other poor people with whom she, a de Tristan, was forced to associate. Her sense of values had become twisted ; her discontent and the shortage of food in her home made her bad tempered, and at times it was unbearable for her to see her mother, ' Minette,' as she affection-ately called her, working so hard without financial results.

Flora's complete lack of education had made her pathetically ambitious. The book learning she herself had missed caused her, throughout her life, to over-emphasize the importance of a formal educa-tion. She bitterly resented the fact that she had never

72 SEVEN WOMEN AGAINST THE WORLD

been taught how to spell the simplest words. In her novel, *Méphis or the Proletarian*, published in 1838, the two chief characters are constantly studying, constantly trying to acquire knowledge ; and when, many years later, her young disciple Eleanore Blanc came to her, Flora arranged the young woman's life on a rigid schedule of reading and self-education.

As a young girl Flora Tristan masked her dissatisfaction with herself and her ignorance behind the arrogant manner which she retained, especially before strangers, as she grew older. In an essay published in *La Sylphide* of January 5, 1845, Jules Janin writes rather cruelly that 'she was unhappy not to be a queen at least somewhere, if she could not be a queen everywhere.'

Her appearance might indeed have excused her apparent vanity, but she was always relatively unaware of her great beauty, her compelling charm, which even her determination verging on hardness could not lessen, and which later made such a strong appeal to the workers of France to whom she lectured. She looked very Spanish : huge dark eyes, and dark curls which surrounded her beautifully shaped face, her splendid high forehead. Her slightly discontented and moody mouth was counteracted by the firmness of her chin. Her face shows that she was a woman who knew exactly what she wanted, though she might never actually get it. She was obviously a human being who might be broken, but who would never bend or give way.

In 1818, when Flora was fifteen and old enough to support herself, her mother moved to Paris. They lived in the rue Fouarre, near the Place Moubert, at the time the worst district in Paris. ' Le quartier souffrant ' it has sometimes been called, ' le zone d'escarpes et des prostituées.'

Flora soon found employment in the lithographic establishment of André Chazal, a young man of about twenty-four. She was quick to learn, and soon coloured valuable lithographs for him. As she was paid by the hour, she sometimes took work home, and Chazal, who was infatuated with her almost as soon as they had met, often came to her room in the evening to help her. He asked her to marry him, and she accepted. They were married in 1821, when she was eighteen years old.

Later, when André's orderly middle-class habits had literally driven her almost mad, Flora pretended that her mother had made her marry him. Throughout her life she dramatized herself to such an extent that her imagination often got the better of her factual memory. She wrote many years afterwards that 'her mother forced her to marry this man whom she neither loved nor respected.'—'As my mother never stopped showing me how grieved she was that she had made me marry him, I have forgiven her.'

Actually, Chazal, dull little man that he was, was probably truthful when he wrote years later with the humility that maddened her : ' she did not feel, or at least she never showed, an unsurmountable feeling of repulsion for me.'

At the time of their marriage Flora herself led André to believe that she cared for him. Perhaps then, too, she was dramatizing herself, perhaps she was being slightly dishonest with herself, or with him. And who could blame her for preferring any marriage, which would give her security, to the terrible poverty she had always known. Whatever her private thoughts, or her own frame of mind, she wrote André passionate letters before their marriage. In her incredible spelling she closes one of them, for instance, with the following words : ' Adieu, ami de mon cœur, au le matin comme il tapelais se cœur, je te cherchais des yeux, ma bouche cherchait la tienne, mes bras cherchait a te sairé sur mon sein, sur ce sein qui n'a connu le plaisir que par toi, . . . mille baisers de flamme sur tes jolis petites laivres.'

74 SEVEN WOMEN AGAINST THE WORLD

During the first year or two of their marriage, when as Flora expressed it, she was still ' trying to become a perfect wife,' she obviously made a desperate effort to adjust herself to normal middle-class life. She tried to control her sharp temper, to be ' bonne avec tout le monde,' to live down her disorganized childhood and early youth. In fact, so Chazal reports, she wanted to reassert herself beyond that, she was striving to be a lady in the snobbish sense of the word. At the beginning of this marriage, Chazal writes, ' her vanity, her desire to achieve a position above our real one, had not yet made her forget her duty.'

Flora stayed with André for four miserable years. On the surface they seemed a peaceful *ménage*. They had two children, a boy and a girl, a modest but comfortable flat in the rue des Fosses-Saint-Germain-des-Près ; André's business was doing well, and on Sunday afternoons the little family could be seen leaving their house for a peaceful walk before the evening meal.

As a matter of fact this little household was moving towards a crisis, which, as far as Flora was concerned, was the starting-point of her independent career. As a very young girl, before she met Chazal, and when the struggle for her daily bread had given her time to think of love, she had longed for a great passion that would make her afraid. ' Faire peur,' was how she herself defined it. These high expectations contrasted cruelly with what André, so exasperatingly precise and unimaginative, had given her.

At the beginning of 1825, when she felt like screaming in rage whenever she saw her husband, Flora began to think of leaving him. For what or how, she had not yet the faintest idea. Divorce had been suppressed again in France in 1816, and a woman who ran away from her husband was considered outside the pale of decent society.

In view of Flora's explosive temperament it is surprising that in a fit of rage she did not simply take

FLORA TRISTAN

the children and leave her flat. Probably the fact that she was going to have another child prevented her from doing anything quite so reckless. Instead, she calmly announced to her husband one day that the younger child, still an infant, needed a change. The elder boy was sent to her mother, and she with the baby and the nurse retired to the country. She never returned to André. After her daughter Aline was born, Flora asked her mother to take the three children, and then she herself made a definite break with her husband.

She was twenty-three when she decided to leave him, and to emancipate herself from this marriage which had become a nightmare to her. She was fully aware of the difficulties she would face ; she knew how hard it would be to support herself, her mother, and her three children. Had she been older and more experienced, she might have hesitated, for the task before her seemed almost impossible.

In the first place, she had never learned a real trade or profession, and besides, as she well knew, it would not be easy to keep any employment if her employer found out that she was a woman who had left her husband and who had no social status. Chazal had been right when he said triumphantly that by deserting him she prepared for 'her rôle as a pariah.' She was an outcast, forced to give false names, to change her address frequently and to live the furtive life of a criminal.

Besides, legally, every centime she earned belonged to her husband, whether she was living with him or not, and it was indeed a victory for her when, several years later, she persuaded the courts to grant her a legal separation from him as far as her income was concerned.

Flora was not to be daunted by the hardship she met when she left Chazal. When she had once moved in any direction she seemed to rush on, driven by

76 SEVEN WOMEN AGAINST THE WORLD

her own primitive force. It must, of course, be remembered, that throughout her childhood she had known the greatest poverty, so that being poor held no unknown terrors for her. Nor did she expect quite such vindictive opposition from Chazal. She had anticipated that he would make her situation difficult, very difficult, but she had underestimated the violent hatred of which he was capable. She was so indifferent herself to what the neighbours might say, she cared so little about respectability as such, that she did not realize how deeply she had wounded André Chazal in his most sensitive spot : his respectability. For fifteen years he did everything he could to turn her into the pariah he had predicted she would become. He pursued her indefatigably with his desire for revenge ; he tried to find out where she was working, so that he could inform her employer that she was an unsuitable person ; he longed to make it impossible for her to live in any decent boarding-house.

Again and again he tried, sometimes successfully and sometimes unsuccessfully, to abduct her children, which legally were still his. The possession of Aline, their daughter, who was born in the country after Flora had left André, became the chief bone of contention between these two angry people. The mother of Paul Gauguin experienced still more upheavals in her childhood than her mother and her grandmother had known before her.

Finally, as Flora had remained undefeated in her purpose in life, as she had supported herself and kept her children, André's anger turned into fury. The climax in their lifelong struggle occurred when one day he followed Flora in the street and shot at her. She was wounded, but soon recovered, and he was sentenced to twenty years' hard labour. Her final release from his tormenting pursuit had not meant a real victory, and she became so notorious after this

FLORA TRISTAN 77

event, that many of her contemporaries forgot everything about her except this scandal.

When she left him she could not foresee the dramatic conclusion of their bitter struggle. At first her life was, in fact, anything but dramatic. She took a job as colourist in another lithograph shop ; and then she became the cashier at a confectioner's. André, however, had already begun to track her down systematically and so she decided to leave France. In 1826 she went to England as a chambermaid to an English family. Very little is known about her first stay in England, though she remained for five years and travelled with her employers in Italy and Switzerland. Her somewhat mysterious attitude towards this period of her life is sometimes attributed to her snobbishness ; it is said that she disliked remembering the humble work she did at this time.

This accusation, however, is most probably unjust, for her hard life had by this time made her wonder about the causes of her misery, and from these considerations it was only a step for a woman like Flora, who was human despite her outward hardness, to regret the injustices suffered by others. Flora began to think and to read.

She was in England towards the end of the Industrial Revolution when the fight for universal male suffrage was beginning in earnest, and shortly before such newspapers as the *Poor Man's Guardian* or the *Pioneer* encouraged the workers to undertake ' economic action ' in the form of strikes and mass demonstrations. No thinking person could have spent the years from 1825–29 in England without becoming acutely conscious of the restlessness which was beginning to spread among the working classes. As yet, Flora remained an observer of this development ; it had not yet occurred to her that she would take any active part in it.

Late in 1829 Flora must have returned to France,

78 SEVEN WOMEN AGAINST THE WORLD

for it is known that during that winter she was staying in a small Paris hotel, where she had registered as Mademoiselle F. Tristan. The man who usually sat next to her when she had her evening meal in the small gloomy dining-room was Captain Zacharie Chabrié. He was the captain of a vessel travelling regularly from France to South America. He asked Flora whether by any chance she was related to the Tristan family in Peru. She denied this, of course, as she was in constant terror of André Chazal's spies, but she managed to learn more about her relatives from Chabrié, and in the course of the conversation he mentioned their address.

She wrote at once to her father's younger brother, for her mother had told her that Don Mariano had been particularly good to him. Then she returned to England, waiting impatiently for the answer from Peru. When it finally reached her, she was somewhat disappointed, for the letter from her uncle contained more affection than money. Still, he did send 2500 francs. So she returned to France—again Chazal was threatening to kidnap Aline, and Flora was needed to prevent this from happening—determined to spend most of this money on a journey to Peru.

On this journey she travelled as Mademoiselle Flora Tristan de Morosco, using one of her father's family names. She hoped, while in Peru, to interest her relatives in herself and her children, so that their future might be secured. This was her conscious reason for going to South America ; her psychological reason was, of course, that she was growing increasingly restless. She was nervous and irritable when she was long in one place. As some women change their lovers, she craved for a change in environment, and by this time life would have seemed dull and empty to her without Chazal's persecutions.

She sailed from Bordeaux on *Le Mexicain.* She was beside herself when she discovered that her old

FLORA TRISTAN

acquaintance, Zacharie Chabrié, was the captain of this
ship, for he would know that she was travelling under
an assumed name and that she had lied to him in
the Paris hotel. She was determined to travel incog-
nito and surprise her relatives, so there was nothing
to do but to take Zacharie into her confidence. These
confidences began a romance which lasted during the
voyage. To Flora, whose love of the dramatic was
becoming more intense as she grew older, the coin-
cidence of meeting him again was in itself romantic.

Her visit to Peru was not particularly successful,
except that it satisfied her desire for travel and to see
the world. Her relatives were somewhat startled when
they met this strange excitable woman. It was unfortunate enough, so they argued, that her father's
marriage had not been a regular one, but at least this
woman could have kept her marital affairs in order.

It roused Flora's feminist instincts when people
expressed surprise, or even disapproval, that she, a
woman, should be travelling alone, and when she
returned to France in 1834 she wrote her first published pamphlet pleading that foreign women should
be well received in other countries : *Necessité de faire
bon accueil aux femmes étrangères.*

Her second pamphlet, too, was concerned with
women ; this time she pleaded for a reintroduction
of divorce in France. It was only natural that Flora,
whose entire life was overshadowed by the injustices
she suffered because she was a woman, should have
approached the social problem from the feminist point
of view. Besides, now that she had begun to study
conditions, the facts increased her ardent feminism.
Women workers in France at the time were receiving
only from sixty to seventy centimes for an eighteen-
hour working day.

Theoretically, too, she believed that women would
in time exert a powerful influence for the good in
society. This idea was not new ; the Saint-Simonites,

80 SEVEN WOMEN AGAINST THE WORLD

for instance, preached that when women's equality with men had been finally recognized by society, the former would regenerate humanity. Flora Tristan never neglected this struggle for the rights of women even later when she had become obsessed with the wish to help the working classes as a whole. A section of her *Union Ouvrière*, which is dedicated to 'men and to women,' deals with the problems of her own sex. In this section of her book she is decades beyond her age in her demands : she objects, for instance, to a double standard of morals, suggesting not that men conform to the monogamous standards imposed on women, but that women should enjoy the same freedom as men. And at a time when suffrage for unpropertied men was not yet established, she urged that women be granted the same legal rights as men.

Flora had a tremendous admiration for Mary Wollstonecraft. She pointed out that 'in 1792 Mary Wollstonecraft expressed the ideas which Saint-Simon taught much later, and which spread so rapidly after the revolution of 1830.' Mary Wollstonecraft's *Vindication of the Rights of Women*, so Flora was convinced, 'was an imperishable work . . . because the happiness of mankind will depend upon the triumph of the cause defended in this book.'

In view of Flora's passionate feminism it is not surprising that for a long time she was greatly attracted by Fourier's social philosophy. He firmly believed in the economic and the personal rights of women. She had been so harassed by her own miserable marriage that when she began to consider social problems she had an exaggerated appreciation of any one who generalized, as Fourier did, that marriage was a hypocritical institution, and that free love was the only proper adjustment of the relation between men and women. ' Can one find even a shadow of justice in the fate which is granted to women ? ' Fourier had asked.

FLORA TRISTAN 81

Flora was not attracted only by Fourier's reforms for women. His optimistic, though unreal and fantastic doctrines at first impressed her as they did many who were experiencing a bitter struggle for existence. With her mind, as her later works show, she saw conditions, and human beings, as they really were. Emotionally, however—and modern psychologists would therefore probably call her a split personality—she was for some time enthusiastic about Fourier's vague pseudo-philosophical teachings. It comforted her to escape from the harsh realities of her life into his belief that all human instincts were fundamentally good and noble ; that, given the proper outlet and surroundings, human society would be reformed, and all would be well with the world.

Later, when she clarified her ideas and realized that the wage earners could ameliorate their situation only by a united effort, she became more critical of Fourier. She admitted that his theories could not achieve any practical results, because ' only associations of the workers themselves can save them from oppression and famine.' Arnold Ruge, at one time an associate of Karl Marx, in his *Three Years in Paris*, records several conversations he had with her about Fourier. ' Fourier,' she said to Ruge, ' had a great name. He had the right to criticize the Revolution and the conduct of our society, but instead he left us these weak fools, who are perpetuating his own mistakes in judgement: his injustice towards the Revolution and towards the work of establishing a free constitution.'

Even while she still took Fourier more or less seriously, however, Flora seems to have given more consideration to the work of Robert Owen, and she was always keenly interested in his New Lanark Colony. With him she advocated peaceful methods of achieving a change in the social structure, but she thought him ' too preoccupied with his belief in the

82 SEVEN WOMEN AGAINST THE WORLD

far-reaching influence of outward environment on human beings.' Flora met Owen when he was in Paris in 1837. This meeting renewed her interest in England. She determined to return there when she had finished a long book she was writing.

This work, her *Pérégrinations d'une Paria*, which appeared in 1838, and was an autobiographical account of her journey to Peru, was her first literary success. Her novel *Mephis* appeared late that same year, and now she was established as a writer. She contributed to various newspapers; she took a flat at No. 100 *bis* rue du Bac; she received her friends; and her home was rapidly becoming a *salon*. Flora, in other words, was on the verge of settling down for the first time in her life.

Soon, however, her usual restlessness asserted itself. A routine existence in one place was unbearable to her. Besides, she was gradually coming to the definite conclusion that she had a social duty to perform. She felt a call; she must contribute actively towards the reform of society. And so, in 1839, after writing a petition to the Chamber to abolish the death sentence, she returned to London to study the work of Owen, John Gray, Abram Combe, and others. Above all, she was interested in the new Chartist Movement, which she called ' the most formidable association which had been organized in the three Kingdoms.' Though she always considered herself a staunch pacifist, who opposed violence in the struggle between the classes, she quotes above the chapter on the Chartists in her book about England their slogan : ' It is better to die by the sword than from hunger.'

She attended several secret Chartist meetings which appealed both to the rational and the romantic side of her nature. She remembered with awe that the members of the early Church, too, had met secretly in crypts, ' dans les caves et les cavernes les premiers

FLORA TRISTAN

83

apôtres réanimessent les chrétiens et leurs paroles étaient plus puissantes que la force des Césars.'

She recorded her experiences in England in her *Promenades dans Londres*, first published in Paris in 1840. This book reflects her clear insight into industrial conditions. She was a pioneer of the hundreds of efficient women investigators who have come after her. She was indefatigable ; she travelled in the industrial districts of the North, bombarding works managers with questions, collecting statistics, comparing living costs and wages in France and in England, taking notes. The first-hand knowledge of conditions among the working classes in England where, so she wrote, ' twenty million proletarians are weeping and suffering,' intensified her fervent wish to do something about it. ' Should one not organize the working classes everywhere,' she pleaded, ' and reveal to them their latent power ? ' And ' this work,' her desire for action prompted her to call her *Union Ouvrière*, ' less of a written work than an action.'

Flora Tristan was extremely thorough in her study of English affairs. She went everywhere where human beings might be oppressed or badly treated. She studied prostitution, insanity, conditions in the prisons. At Bedlam she met a mad Frenchman named Chabrier. Though he spelled his name with an *r* at the end, she was struck by the similarity between his name and that of the sea captain she had known on her way to Peru. Coincidences always made her highly expectant, they seemed to rouse all that was mystical in her character.

The madman, pathetically happy at hearing his native language, took some straw with which he had been playing and made a cross of it. ' Take it,' he said to her, ' I am the representative of your God : The Messiah whose coming was predicted by Jesus Christ. Take this cross, wear it, and proclaim the new Law to the world.'

84 SEVEN WOMEN AGAINST THE WORLD

Flora was deeply moved. She took the cross and later wrote : ' I shall achieve the work which he indicated. I shall cause all servitude to cease in the world ; I shall free women from the bondage of men ; the poor from the bondage of the rich ; and human souls from the bondage of sin.'

Flora's fanaticism was undoubtedly stimulated to an abnormal pitch by this experience at Bedlam. From that time onwards she thought of her work in terms of a mission. Eleanore Blanc, in her short biographical sketch of Flora, speaks of her ' apostolic life.'

Again, however, that strange differentiation between her emotional fantasies about her work and the work itself became apparent. The incident at Bedlam, and her reaction to it, might make it seem that her mind had become unbalanced. But the contrary was true. She saw things that mattered more clearly than ever before, and her flights of imagination remained her private luxury, which did not hinder her serious work in the least.

When she returned to Paris, utterly obsessed by the subject of her book, Chazal again interrupted her, and this time seriously. For though she was not fatally wounded, it was a shock to this highly strung woman to be shot at in the street in broad daylight. The publicity she attracted by this final and terrible dénouement of her unhappy marriage, and André Chazal's sentence to twenty years' hard labour, weighed down upon her heavily. Never for a moment, however, did she allow this personal depression to interfere with her work.

Even before *l'Union Ouvrière* was published, she began travelling about France holding meetings and urging the workers to form *sociétiés de compagnonnage*, which were the forerunners of modern trade unions. She met with great opposition. ' Almost the entire world is against me,' she wrote, ' men because I am

FLORA TRISTAN

demanding the emancipation of women ; the propertied classes because I am demanding the emancipation of the wage earners.'

She did not exaggerate the fierceness of the attacks which were launched against her. The newspapers called her 'a revolutionary blue-stocking,' or an 'apostle in petticoats,' and the police hounded her down wherever she spoke. On one occasion a woman, the owner of a house of ill-repute, approached her on behalf of the police in the hopes of compromising her. Once, when she was holding a meeting in Lyon, the police came to the hotel where she was staying and searched her possessions for subversive literature.

Naturally, this antagonism only encouraged a fighter of Flora's temperament. She went on with her meetings and with the writing of her book. She was then confronted with the serious problem of having it published. No publisher would accept so revolutionary a manuscript. So she decided to print it herself. To do so, funds were needed, and she set out on the arduous task of collecting money. She enraged Lafitte, the banker, of whom Karl Marx wrote that 'he betrayed the secret of the revolution,' by taking his Liberalism seriously and asking him for a contribution. Needless to say, she did not get it ; instead, he dismissed her rudely.

She was more fortunate when she appealed to the intellectuals of the day, and Béranger, Eugene Sue, Ponsard, and George Sand were among the people who helped her to publish her book. George Sand, however, was more in sympathy with Flora Tristan's ideas than with her personality. 'She was never very sympathetic to me,' George Sand confessed, 'despite her courage and her convictions. She was always too vain.'

Flora herself hated asking strangers for money, but her faith in her book made her do so. 'To find

86 SEVEN WOMEN AGAINST THE WORLD

three people willing to give,' she wrote, dramatizing herself a little as usual, ' I often had to see twenty, and I went everywhere on foot, and this was difficult. But the love of my cause is so great within me that my fatigue cannot deter me. What tires me, however, is to meet indifference—especially among those [the working classes] whom I am serving. Nevertheless, despite everything, I feel calm and contented. I know that I am doing something worth while, which must lead to good results, and this thought is comforting.'

Many of the men and women who had helped her to publish her book had expected that it would be an exalted and impractical appeal on behalf of the wage earners. When she called on her supporters, Flora had made a confused and extremely intense impression on them. Like many brilliant orators, and there is no question that she had unusual gifts as a public speaker, Flora often appeared loose-minded, a dreamer, when she talked to one person. Besides, strangers now connected her in their minds with the scandal André Chazel had created by shooting her, and this *crime passionelle* did not seem to fit in with her rôle of social reformer.

When *l'Union Ouvrière* appeared in 1843 it caused considerable surprise. The book begins clearly and concisely. Addressed to the workers themselves, it is in simple language; she never imposes on them her great knowledge of social problems.

' For twenty-five years,' Flora Tristan tells the wage earners, both men and women, ' the most intelligent and devoted men have consecrated their lives to your cause.' In a footnote she then mentioned the names of Saint-Simon, Owen, Fourier, Pierre Leroux, Louis Blanc, Proudhon, and others. ' There is nothing more to say,' she continues, ' nothing more to write . . . there is only one thing to do : for you to act in accordance with the rights included in the Charter ; and it is for you, for you alone, to act.'

FLORA TRISTAN

There is no question but that, as Jules Puech, Flora Tristan's able biographer, declares, *l'Union Ouvrière* ' was the most definite summary of a revolutionary catechism which had yet appeared (in France), for this work, in principle, and without contradicting the gentle philanthropy of its pacifist author, first propounded the subject of the class war.'

Before Flora Tristan's time, reformers had tried to promote various types of mutual aid societies amongst the workers, societies which benefited them during periods of illness, accident, or unemployment. The aim of these plans, which undoubtedly represented a certain progress, was to relieve the suffering of the poor in times of stress. Flora Tristan, with rare insight in an age when even welfare work was considered almost revolutionary, realized that these temporary measures could be of no lasting value whatsoever. She rejected these societies, and taught that only by uprooting the causes of the workers' poverty and oppression could they derive any lasting benefits.

Her realization that the workers must unite before they can accomplish anything at all has stood the test of history. This idea, as has been said, was her great contribution to the social development of France, a contribution which was taken seriously by such men as Karl Marx and Friedrich Engels. In their *Collected Works*, Friedrich Engels attacks a critic, who in turn has objected to her demand that the workers of France should co-operate.

Flora Tristan was a realist, furthermore, in her belief that the influence of the workers' union should be based on the economic power of money. 'The union of workers . . . will have a real influence based on the power of money,' she wrote. She knew that there were between seven and eight million industrial workers in France. She calculated, therefore, that each of these workers could easily be persuaded to con-

88 SEVEN WOMEN AGAINST THE WORLD

tribute two francs a year to the cause of their unity; and that this would mean fourteen million francs a year as a fighting fund for the association. This hope was not a realistic conception. She was too much of an idealist; she could not admit, even to herself, that there might be some or many workers among the seven million who would have no desire to help themselves by supporting the union. Nor did she remember that employers were free to dismiss the workers at any time, and thus make it impossible for them to continue their contributions to the mutual fund.

If, as Flora Tristan firmly believed, it had been possible for the workers to collect sufficient funds for them to fight the propertied classes with economic weapons, her hope that 'their union alone would be enough and that no force would be necessary' might have been fulfilled. History has shown, however, that economic weapons—quite apart from the fact that they are impracticable and independable—are not strong enough to defend the rights of the working classes, but her idea of the unity necessary before these rights can be acquired has been fully justified.

She urged the workers of France to stop quarrelling among themselves, and to adjust the differences between members of the various guilds and trades. All working men and women, she preached, should co-operate in order ' to attain from the propertied classes the right to live.' And more than that, she foresaw the urgent need for workers in various countries to unite, regardless of national bonds; she appealed to them to fight for a common aim, 'regardless of individual distinction of trade and of country.' She observed ' with grief,' for instance, that for religious reasons ' O'Connell was preventing the workers of Ireland from fraternizing with their English brothers.'

Flora was never so impractical as to think that her teachings would reach the workers merely through her

FLORA TRISTAN 89

book. As soon as it was published, she again set out on a tour of enlightenment. She held meetings in Dijon, Lyon, Marseilles, Toulouse, and many other cities and towns. She reached Bordeaux towards the end of September 1844. Here she was taken seriously ill. The doctors diagnosed her attack as a severe cerebral hæmorrhage. She died on the fourteenth of November, and she was buried in Bordeaux.

The workers of the city collected funds to erect a simple tombstone in her memory. ' To the memory of Madame Flora Tristan, the author of *l'Union Ouvrière,*' it said, ' from the Grateful Workers.' And under this sentence were carved the words : ' *Liberté —Egalité—Fraternité—Solidarité.*'

Perhaps had Flora Tristan lived to witness or to participate in the revolutionary events of 1848, she might have changed her mind about the form which the workers' struggle would assume. As it was, though her ideas were far beyond other teachings of her own age, she did not see clearly how the working classes would eventually use the united strength she had urged them to acquire. In the unity she preached, however, she gave them the basis for future action. The men and women of Bordeaux showed a profound understanding of her achievement when they added the word ' solidarity ' to those other words which, before her time, had been the symbol of French liberty. *Liberté—Egalité—Fraternité,* and now *Solidarité* as well.

IV

LOUISE MICHEL (1830-1905)

LOUISE MICHEL's life was curiously connected with all the important revolutionary movements of the nineteenth century, and she was brought up by her grandfather who had taken an active part in the French Revolution of 1789. She was born in 1830, shortly before the insurrection of the Paris workers ; she was mature enough fully to appreciate the significance of the uprisings of 1848. She fought on the barricades to defend the Paris Commune of 1871, which has been called ' the first dress rehearsal in world history of the Socialist revolution of the working class.' She died in 1905, not long before the outbreak of the first Russian Revolution which marked the beginning of the far-reaching social upheavals of our own century.

Louise Michel was a highly educated woman, her knowledge of many subjects, as Henri Barbusse says, was encyclopædic, but she was not what modern Socialists would call a ' trained Marxist.' She was not always a clear thinker, and she never made a real distinction between socialism and anarchy. ' We are all fighting a common enemy,' she once declared in this connexion. ' For myself I am not concerned with these differences, for, let me repeat, I side with all those who are attacking the damnable edifice of our old society : I side with all of them, whether their weapons are pick-axes, bombs, or fire.'

This passage shows that, unlike many women in history who have shared her profound humanity, a humanity verging on tenderness towards helpless creatures, Louise Michel rejected parliamentary reform.

92 SEVEN WOMEN AGAINST THE WORLD

She was convinced that the rich would not surrender their power and privileges unless they were forced to do so. She believed that oppression would cease only if the oppressed used force. She hated violence, but she accepted its application as an inevitable step towards social progress. She was, in other words, the first great woman revolutionary who actively preached the class war, and who took part in it herself.

Many women—Joan of Arc, for instance—have inspired men to fight more valiantly for their cause. Louise Michel, on the other hand, fought side by side with men as their comrade and their equal. 'Do try to remember,' she said impatiently to her solicitous surgeon when she had been badly wounded in the ear by a man who shot at her in a Socialist meeting, 'do try to remember that I am a fighter and not a woman.'

Her last portrait, drawn when she was over seventy, does indeed look like that of a man who has been a fighter throughout his life. She wore her hair a bit longer than was usual among the emancipated women of her generation, but the rest of her head is extremely masculine. The lower part of her face reminds one of portraits of Frederick the Great; her high, not beautifully shaped forehead resembles pictures of old generals, and her very long and ugly nose recalls Napoleon's remark that ' when he wanted good headwork done he always chose a man, if suitable otherwise, with a long nose.'

Her figure was thin and upright; there were no soft curves about Louise Michel. Teophil Zolling, a German journalist, who interviewed her in 1880, says that 'in contrast to her mother she was ugly, but she did not strike me as really ugly if I tried to forget that she was a woman '; and Louise herself, in her *Memoirs*, recalls one night in Paris when a man, hoping for an adventure, followed her in the street.

LOUISE MICHEL 93

Finally, she turned and spoke to him, and he was so startled by her deep masculine voice and by the oath she uttered that he ran away horrified, thinking she was a man disguised as a woman.

Though she became one of the most uncomprising revolutionaries of the nineteenth century, not excepting the Russians, she was not involved in any active service for her cause during the first forty years of her life.

'My life,' she writes, 'was divided into two distinct periods, which were entirely different. The first consisted of dreams and of study ; the second only of events. It was as though the aspirations of the period of calm came to life during the period of active conflict.'

Louise Michel was born on the twenty-ninth of May, 1830, in the village of Vroncourt, near Domrémy, in the Haute-Marne. The circumstances of her birth were somewhat irregular, but her childhood was unusually happy. She was the illegitimate child of Marianne Michel, a woman of peasant stock employed as a maid on the estate of the Dehamis family. Both father and son were at home, and there was some discussion as to which of them was the father of this child. The son, who is generally believed to have been Louise's father, left home to manage a farm of his own, and Louise was brought up by her grandfather, Etienne-Charles Dehamis, a cultured, kindly, and understanding old man, a lawyer by profession, a Rationalist, a humanitarian, and a passionate believer in the ' rights of men.'

Louise's grandmother was as enlightened as was her husband, and the child was brought up and educated as carefully and quite as affectionately as though she had been a legitimate member of the family. At the same time, and this reflects Dehamis' and his wife's remarkable understanding, Louise's mother was never excluded from the discussion of any

94 SEVEN WOMEN AGAINST THE WORLD

problem concerning her daughter's upbringing. To Louise, who was deeply attached to her mother, this somewhat strange domestic situation seemed the most natural thing in the world.

Dehamis gave Louise a most thorough and systematic education. He had infinite patience ; he was always ready to answer her questions. ' Sometimes,' she wrote of him later, ' he was as ironical as Voltaire, the great master of his generation ; in other moods he was as gay and as witty as Molière ; he would explain to me the many different kinds of books which we read together.'

Dehamis realized that his granddaughter was an exceptionally gifted and versatile child. He encouraged her interest in music ; he was pleased when she made herself a lute out of an old board and some discarded guitar strings. He criticized her poetry ; she began to write verse when she was very young. He helped her when, before she was ten, she wanted to write a world history, which she called *Une Histoire Universelle*.

Above all, Louise's grandfather was relieved to see that this healthy, active child was by no means a confirmed blue-stocking. He never objected to her wild boyish games ; her love of adventure. She would roam about the countryside for hours with Jules, her constant companion, a cousin of her own age. Occasionally old Dehamis reminded her that they should play together more as equals, for Louise was consistently the leader of their expeditions.

The stories which her grandfather told her of the great French Revolution held her imagination. She and Jules played at uprisings ; at fighting for causes, at being martyrs. They often piled wood up high in the courtyard of the old manor-house and pretended that they were being burned at the stake. They sang lustily as the imaginary flames rose round them.

LOUISE MICHEL 95

' One day,' Louise remembered, ' when we were
singing as we mounted the scaffold, my grandfather
suggested that it would be better to mount it in
silence. Then when we stood at the top, he said, we
were again to proclaim the principles for which we
were dying ; so that is what we always did after
that.'

Political problems took possession of Louise's
young mind as soon as she was really conscious of
anything. Her great hero was Victor Hugo, who
before 1830 had been an ardent Legitimist, but who
was now becoming an extreme Liberal. Louise sent
him some of her first poems ; he thanked the little
girl and told her to go on writing. Her admiration
for him persisted for years, and she felt an almost
personal pride when he later became an ardent
democratic Republican.

As a child, her days of extreme political interest
were often interrupted by an intense love of Nature,
by exciting tales about travels or distant countries.
In common with many completely irreligious people,
Louise believed neither in a deity nor in a future life.
Instead, her imagination was stimulated by fantasies
about unseen places on earth.

Her grandfather understood the strange combination of romanticism and harsh realism in her nature.
He made small wooden ships for her ; she sailed them
on the pond, satisfying her longing for the sea which
she had never seen. It is a tragic fact that the
first time she visited a foreign country it was to the
penal colony of New Caledonia as a prisoner. She
often looked back not without sadness to her childhood
when she had looked forward to a thrilling life of
adventure. She wrote :

' Pour mes premiers jouets il me fit des bateaux,
De beaux bateaux pontés ayant haubans et hunes
Et dans la pierre ronde on les mettait a flots,
A travers les crapauds monstres aux teintes brunes

96 SEVEN WOMEN AGAINST THE WORLD

Qui sur les ponts parfois faisaient d'énormes bonds.
C'était pres du vieil orme et des ruches d'abeilles.
Des roses de Provins aux pétales vermeilles
Etudaient leurs rameaux sur les résédas blonds.

.   .   .   .

Oh ! Combien tout enfant j'ai vu de blanches voiles
S'en aller sur les flots dans mes rêves les soir,
J'en voyais un toujours, qui seul sous les étoiles
Semblait un grand oiseau blanc à l'horizon noir.
Comme je la peignais avec sa vive allure,
Et la fière forêt de sa haute mature,
Mon grand-père me dit : Nous ferons ton bateau
Avec du cœur de chêne et ce sera très beau.
C'est une frégate. . . .'

Louise Michel wrote poems until she was a very old woman ; she remained acutely conscious of beauty in any form, but in the end she became a practising realist. Her social consciousness was so strong that it pushed aside her romantic instincts. The injustice of the society into which she was born obsessed her, and the urge to contribute towards a change of the social system finally ruled her life, and made her heroic. She herself did not believe in heroism. 'Heroism simply does not exist,' she declared, ' it is nothing but a sense of duty and a revolutionary passion, and these are not virtues any more than love or fanaticism are virtues.'

People who saw the gentleness with which she cared for sick animals often thought her sentimental or soft. And when, during the Commune, she left a protected spot behind the barricade to rescue a kitten, some of her comrades thought her mad. Actually, she saved the kitten because instinctively, without weighing the costs, she always helped the weak. And she was not sentimental even as a child. On the contrary, she showed unusual hardness towards those whom she considered enemies of human rights and justice.

LOUISE MICHEL

97

She was deeply upset by the cruelty with which some of the peasants near Vroncourt treated their animals, but, unlike most tender hearted children, she was not satisfied to bind up their wounds, to beg the men to be kinder to these helpless creatures. She was never content with humanitarian gestures. Her rebellious instincts were too strong, and she ' wished that the animal could revenge itself, that the dog would bite the man who was beating him so cruelly ; that the horse, bleeding under the whip, would throw off the inhuman brute who was riding him.'

Though her life with her grandparents was happy, Louise could never quite forget these moments when she had witnessed human cruelty. She began to think when she was very young, and the realization of the injustices of life, the unnecessary cruelties of human society, haunted her always. ' Happiness is a vision on some distant planet,' she once wrote, ' it is an ideal which cannot be attained in this world.' She was a gay child, and at times she was boisterous, but already she was developing the innate sadness which never left her as long as she lived. But her sadness was never tinged by defeatism, and it is strange that, meeting her as an old woman, so many people thought her hard and grim.

Her childhood ended very abruptly when she was in her teens. Her grandparents died within a few years of each other, and her father, Laurent Dehamis, came back to the manor at Vroncourt bringing his wife, a most unpleasant and petty woman, with him. Madame Dehamis tried to make Louise conscious of the irregularity of her birth. She strenuously objected to the child's position in the house ; she was furious when she heard the villagers call her ' Mademoiselle Dehamis ' as they had always done. An attempt was made to relegate Louise's mother to the servant's quarters. As a result, Louise's great affection for her mother developed, as Madame Boyer so rightly says,

7

98 SEVEN WOMEN AGAINST THE WORLD

into a ' cult.' Throughout the many years she later spent in prison, or in exile, her mother was her greatest concern.

Laurent Dehamis soon realized that it would be impossible to keep Louise at home, and she was sent to a good school at Chaumont, where she was educated as a schoolmistress. She passed her examinations brilliantly, and took a post at Adeloncourt, near Vroncourt, so that she could be near her mother who was living in the village.

Louise was teaching at Audeloncourt when the *coup d'état* of 1852 ushered in the Second Empire. For the first time she had an opportunity of courageously defending the Republicanism her grandfather had instilled into her. She created an unpleasant sensation when she had the children in her form sing the Marseillaise ; she chalked Republican slogans on the houses of the town ; she continued openly to post letters to Victor Hugo, who was then in exile. She attacked Napoleon III whenever she had a chance. Fear was unknown to her.

She occasionally contributed to the newspapers in Chaumont, and she once got into very serious trouble for an article indirectly attacking the Empire. ' When Domitian reigned,' this article began, ' he banished the philosophers and the scholars from Rome ; he increased the Pretorian Guard ; reestablished the games at the Capitol, and people adored the merciful Emperor while at the same time they hoped that he would be stabbed to death. For some the apotheosis comes before, for some it comes afterwards ! That is all. We are living in Rome in the year A.D. 95.'

She was summoned to the Prefect of Police, who told her that if she were older she might be sent to the penal colony at Cayenne for daring to write such an article. She replied that if he assumed that she meant Napoleon III, he, too, would be insulting the

LOUISE MICHEL

Emperor and a new Prefect of Police might be appointed to his post. She was so obviously fearless that the Prefect was made uneasy ; he dismissed her without another word.

From that time onwards people in the district admired or hated her, according to their attitude towards the Second Empire, but no one was eager to be seen with her. This did not affect Louise in the least. She was never a sociable creature, and she had one friend—Julie L. she calls her in her *Memoirs*—and her mother, and she did not need other companionship. She wanted only to go to Paris where she could be closer to the illegal Republican movements working towards the overthrow of Napoleon.

Finally, in 1856, she was offered a post at Mademoiselle Vollier's school for young ladies at 14 rue du Chateau-d'Eau. Her friend, Julie, too, was engaged to teach there, but they saw less of each other in Paris, for Louise could not rouse her friend's interest in politics, and to her they meant everything.

Louise's salary at Mademoiselle Vollier's establishment was very small. Her grandfather had left her a considerable *dot*, thinking that she would stay at the manor-house at Vroncourt until she was married, but now she was penniless except for what she earned. To support her mother, she gave drawing and music lessons to private pupils in the evenings. She was badly paid, for she had no talent or desire to make money. She was always poor, and when she was dying of pneumonia as an old woman the last five francs she owned in the world were spent on the oxygen ordered by the physician.

Paris during the Second Empire must have been a startling experience to young provincials, especially if they were poor and Republican in spirit like Louise. There was such tremendous luxury side by side with such terrible poverty ; morals were lax among the rich and powerful, who wanted, above all, to enjoy

100 SEVEN WOMEN AGAINST THE WORLD

themselves. Every one was reading the novels of Paul de Kock. Money and financial speculations were dominating society ; bankers were beginning to replace the aristocracy as leaders of society. Modern capitalism, as we understand this term to-day, was developing rapidly.

Louise was not startled for long. Her great intellectual curiosity caused her to think about these conditions rather than to be annoyed by them. Apart from her regular work, she took courses in chemistry and physics. Science and liberty were two words she liked to associate ; she always made a conscious effort to move away from that emotional type of revolutionary found especially among the women of her generation. When Claude Bernard's *Introduction to the Study of Experimental Medicine* appeared in 1865, she welcomed this revolutionary contribution to science with profound respect, and her own early occupation with science gave her a curious feeling of security and of hope. ' How good it was to study these sciences,' she remembered years later, ' one could breathe freely in a quiet little corner even in this Second Empire.'

She belonged to the secret Republican Clubs in the *Quartier Latin*, where she met many of Blanqui's disciples, and she attended study circles at the famous Republican meeting-place in the rue Hauteville. She associated not only with the more extreme Blanquists but with mild Republicans as well, for before the fall of Napoleon III all the groups opposed to him were closely associated, regardless of their views as to the kind of Republic they hoped would succeed the Second Empire. At this time Louise knew such men as Jules Claude Favre, who was later Minister of Foreign Affairs in the Thiers Republic which she so bitterly hated.

In her own mind Louise always connected the word Republic with the social revolution ; she was

LOUISE MICHEL

excited and moved when Karl Marx founded the First International of Working Men's Associations in 1861. She never doubted that the proletarian revolution would eventually come, that it would finally be victorious; but for the moment she was so occupied with her loathing of Napoleon III that she was, of course, willing to co-operate with any one who shared her feeling towards his régime. She vaguely hoped that to remove Napoleon would definitely end the Empire, and she often thought of Victor Hugo's lines :

> ' Harmodius, c'est l'heure,
> Tu peux tuer cette homme avec tranquillité.'

She was always confused about the revolutionary methods in which she believed. She approved of any sensational act of violence, without seeing its possible effects. In 1883, for instance, when a group of German anarchists wanted to bomb a large national monument and a number of German rulers who were unveiling it, she welcomed this plan as a great deed—a deed which would prepare the way for German Socialism.

When she was older and more experienced, and after she had seen many men die on the barricades, Louise Michel still believed in that futile method which modern revolutionaries call ' individual terror.' Later, she had rationalized this point of view, and she declared that too many lives were sacrificed when the people as a whole took part in active revolt, and that therefore ' it would be better if a few courageous individuals sacrificed themselves and, at their own risk, committed acts of violence which would terrorize the government and the bourgeoisie.'

Considering her regular and her private teaching, her preoccupation with theoretical and practical political problems, her attendance at the Clubs, her scientific studies and her reading, it is amazing, in the years she spent in Paris, that Louise Michel found time to write poetry and several novels. As the

102 SEVEN WOMEN AGAINST THE WORLD

titles of her novels indicate, they were all political: *Le Batârd Imperial, La Claque-Dents*, or *Les Microbes humains*. For her conception of fiction, too, was revolutionary. She strongly objected to the slogan ' l'art pour l'art,' advocating, on the contrary, that ' every artist must have a social mission, and every work of art must reflect political action.'

Louise's intellectual pursuits were put aside for several decades when the hostilities began between France and Prussia in 1870. War was declared on the nineteenth of July. After the first minor French defeats, patriotic feeling was rampant in France. Nationalism was further stimulated when the foreign army began to march on to Paris. Blanqui's famous slogan, ' Le Patrie en danger,' reflects the extent to which democratic Frenchmen as well as reactionaries were affected by this patriotic fervour.

In the minds of most Republicans the invasion of French territory was deeply resented ; nationalism identified itself for them with the political beliefs taught at the time of the Convention after the great Revolution. Saving France at this time meant saving the Republic which was to come. Republicans organized committees of vigilance, which were especially strong in Paris.

Louise, usually accompanied by her greatest friend Marie Ferré, a sister of Theophile Ferré, the young revolutionary, went regularly to the meetings of the committee in Montmartre, in the Chaussée Clignan-court. Louise realizing, as Madame Boyer points out, that the time for mere civic courage had passed, was already determined to fight on the barricades fo rher principles. She bought an infantry uniform and joined the Paris crowd which marched to the Hôtel de Ville demanding arms. Jules Favre, who later became one of the Communardes' bitterest enemies, was so impressed by this scene, that he embraced Louise, Theophile Ferré, and Rigaud, another of her friends and fellow-fighters, and called them his ' dear children.'

Early in September, after Prussia's victory at Sedan, it became obvious that France would ultimately be defeated in this war. The Republic was declared after a revolt in Paris on September 4. A provisional Government for National Defence was declared ; Gambetta was entrusted with reorganizing the Army ; General Trochu was appointed Governor of Paris. From the very beginning the Republican Government was made uneasy by the National Guard in Paris, for these battalions of citizens included many Internationalists, Blanquists, and democratic elements generally. ' This Republic,' as Karl Marx pointed out, ' did not really overthrow the throne, it merely stepped into the place it vacated. It was proclaimed, not as a social conquest, but as a measure of national defence.'

The revolutionaries of Paris were aware of the Government's mistrust of them ; they knew that men like Thiers and Favre wanted to disarm the National Guard. During the siege of Paris, Louise Michel and her associate watched the Government from day to day. ' During the siege,' she writes, ' I spent my happiest hours at our Committees ; we lived somewhat in the future, we were happy . . . to be occupied with the intense struggle for liberty.'

Louise was fully aware that the Republican Government was waiting to crush the rebellious element in Paris. She was prepared to be arrested at any moment. ' I kept an old revolver next to me on my desk,' she remembered ; ' often by picking it up at an opportune moment I stopped the police from coming in . . .'

Blanqui was struggling in vain to establish a more democratic Government, but the Prussians were pressing forward and new defeats made it impossible to concentrate on internal governmental affairs.

104 SEVEN WOMEN AGAINST THE WORLD

Gambetta's armies were not successful, and a final French defeat was imminent. On October 31, 1870, battalions of the National Guard, led by Flourens, marched on the Hôtel de Ville, still insisting that the new Republic should not agree to an armistice. If the Prussians marched into Paris, the agitated crowd realized, all hope of a real Republic in the future was lost. Shouts of ' Vive la Commune ' were heard at this demonstration, and Flourens was arrested on the spot and accused of treason against the new Republic.

On January 8, Paris surrendered to the Prussians. The siege of Paris was over. The forts were handed over, the regular French army was disarmed, and the troops became prisoners of war. The National Guard, however, refused to surrender its arms and munitions, and it is significant of the respect these untrained soldiers inspired that the Prussians did not take away their weapons by force.

Thiers and his Government, now established at Versailles, were, however, determined to destroy the National Guard. The elections to the National Assembly, which had occurred on February 8, had returned a majority in favour of the Government, so that the Cabinet was sure of public support throughout France. The Government sent troops to Paris to disband the National Guard. The resistance was tremendous, and the Government troops were defeated in the Montmartre district.

The Paris Commune was declared on the eighteenth of March. ' The proletarians of Paris,' the proclamation of the Commune announced, ' in the midst of the defeats and betrayals of the ruling class, have come to understand that they must save the situation by taking the conduct of public affairs into their own hands. . . . They have realized that it is their highest duty and their absolute right to make themselves the masters of their own fates and to seize the power of the Government.'

LOUISE MICHEL

A Central Committee of the National Guard became the Provisional Government of Paris. In our own century, workers in a similar position of power would probably have maintained the dictatorship of this Provisional Government. In the nineteenth century and especially in France, however, the democratic tradition was so strong that the Central Committee of the National Guard appealed almost at once to the population of Paris, and a general election established a representative Government of the city. In the twentieth century, furthermore, this Provisional Government would probably have marched on to Versailles, would have taken the initiative after the Republican Government's defeat in Montmartre, and an attempt would have been made to bring the members of the Thiers Cabinet back to Paris as prisoners. If this had been done, the Commune might have persisted much longer than it did.

As it was, the Commune, which lasted only a little over two months—it was finally defeated by the Thiers Government in May—brought about tremendous changes in Paris. 'On the 30th of March,' as Friedrich Engels writes, 'the Commune abolished conscription and the standing army, and all military forces except the National Guard, to which all citizens capable of bearing arms were to belong. It remitted all rents from October 1870 to 1871, such rent as had already been paid to be placed to the account of future payments ; it returned gratis all goods of necessitous persons pledged in the municipal pawnshops. The same day the election of foreigners to the Commune was endorsed and their right to function was confirmed, since it was declared " the banner of the Commune is that of the world Republic." ' On the 1st of April it was decided that the highest salary of a functionary of the Commune, whether a member or otherwise, was not to exceed 6,000 francs a year. On the following day the separation of Church and State

106 SEVEN WOMEN AGAINST THE WORLD

was declared, all State payments for religious purposes were stopped, and all ecclesiastical property was converted into national property. As a consequence of this, on the 8th of April all religious symbols, dogmas, prayers—in short, "all things appertaining to the sphere of the individual conscience"—were ordered to be banished from the schools, an order which was gradually carried out. On the 6th the guillotine was fetched out by the 137th battalion of the National Guard and publicly burned with popular acclamation. On the 18th the Commune ordered the column on the Place Vendôme, which had been constructed by Napoleon I after the war of 1809 out of captured cannon, to. be overthrown as a monument of chauvinism and international rivalry. This was accomplished on the 16th of May. On the 16th of April the Commune ordered that all factories and workshops not working be registered, and ordered plans for their being run by the workmen hitherto engaged in them, who were to be formed into co-operative societies for the purpose. Furthermore, these societies were to be amalgamated into one great co-operative organization. On the 20th they abolished the Labour Exchange, which, since the Second Empire, had been the monopoly of certain scoundrels appointed by the police—exploiters of the worst kind. The matter was henceforward placed under the control of the mayors of the twenty arrondissements of Paris. On the 20th of April the Commune decreed the abolition of pawnshops as being incompatible with the right of workmen to their tools and to credit. On the 5th of May it ordered the destruction of the chapel erected in expiation of the execution of Louis XVI.'

Louise Michel was an active defender of the Commune from the beginning to the end. On March 18 she was a member of the 61st battalion of the National Guard, and when this battalion was resting, her fierce energy prompted her to join others

LOUISE MICHEL

for hours or days at a time. Her description of the 18th of March reflects her intense excitement.

'At dawn we heard the alarm signal ; we prepared for the bayonet charge, knowing that an army was ready for the battle.

'We were ready to die for liberty.

'We were exhilarated, our feet did not seem to touch the ground. Paris had risen. . . . Suddenly I saw my mother by my side and I felt a terrible anxiety ; worried, she had come to find me ; all the women had come to join us on the barricades ; I don't know how they got there.

'As soon as General Lecomte ordered his soldiers to open fire on the crowd, a non-commissioned officer left the ranks, and, standing before his company, he shouted louder than Lecomte had shouted : "Begin the Mutiny." The soldiers obeyed him. This non-commissioned officer was Verdaguerre who, for this action, was shot in Versailles a few months later.

'The Revolution had begun.'

Louise remained entirely calm during the street fighting which followed. She felt impersonal, like a machine which was running its inevitable course. 'The first time one defends one's cause with arms,' she wrote, 'one sees the struggle so clearly that one seems to be a bullet oneself.'

Her only worry during the Commune was her mother, whom she saw but rarely. 'During the entire Commune,' she wrote later, 'I only spent one night with my poor mother. I never went to bed ; I slept, when I had time, anywhere I happened to be. Many of the others did the same. Every one who wanted freedom gave everything he had.'

The defeat of the Commune in May was probably the most terrible experience of her life. During the last days of the Commune, when the Versailles Army was already in Paris, and when some of her comrades committed suicide in abject despair, Louise fought on.

108 SEVEN WOMEN AGAINST THE WORLD

She might easily have escaped, but to run away now would have been unthinkable to her. It never occurred to her that she might contribute more to freedom by living than by dying. She was imbued with the old-fashioned sense of duty for its own sake. She was among the last fighters in the Montmartre Cemetery and in the Chaussée Clignancourt. Her fellow-fighters urged her to stay with them : ' Come with us,' one of them said to her, ' you were with . us on the first day, you must remain with us on the last.'

Louise was in Montmartre when the massacre of the Communardes, in which about 25,000 men, women, and children were killed, began. She was knocked down, but managed to get away from the terrible street fighting. Again she might have escaped, but now anxiety for her mother made her go home. She knew the police would be searching for her, and she was sure that if they found her mother alone, the old woman would be taken as a hostage by the Government troops. This had happened, but Madame Michel was released when Louise gave herself up as a prisoner. She was taken to the Sartory prison in the pouring rain. Later she was moved to the prison at Versailles. She awaited her trial.

Her great friend Ferré, who had held an important post during the Commune and who was shot as a traitor with many others, had refused to defend himself when he was tried. ' I refuse to defend myself before men like you,' he had said to his judges. ' Have me taken back to my cell. As you have the upper hand at present, strike. That is good advice which I am giving you. Your turn will come later. We have excellent memories.' Ferré underestimated Louise Michel's absolute devotion to their common cause. He was still afraid that, humane as she was—every one already called her ' La bonne Louise '—she would be too gentle with her enemies. Unfortunately he did not live to hear about her trial, which occurred on the 16th of December 1871.

Though she had suffered the most acute discomforts in prison for over six months, she was, as *Le Voleur* reported, entirely calm and self-possessed when she came into court. ' I do not wish to defend myself,' she declared at once, ' I do not wish any one else to defend me. I belong entirely to the social revolution, and I accept full responsibility for everything I have done. I accept this responsibility without restrictions.'

She expected a death sentence ; she resented the fact that her life might be spared merely because she was a woman. ' It seems,' she declared, ' that the only rights granted to a heart which beats for freedom is a piece of lead in the shape of a bullet. If that is so, I want my rights. . . . If you let me live,' she said in her clear deep voice, ' I shall never cease to shout vengeance on you who have killed my brothers. . . . If you are not cowards, you will kill me.'

Her judges, however, were indeed cowards and afraid that public opinion might be roused against them if they executed this woman. Instead, she was sentenced to banishment in the terrible penal colony of New Caledonia. When asked whether she wanted to appeal against this sentence, she firmly declined, but she did admit that she would have preferred death. She had read about the French penal colonies.

She spent a ghastly year at the prison at d'Aubherne, for she was not sent out to New Caledonia until August 1873. She was very near despair, but as the train transporting the prisoners to Marseilles passed through a small town, a workman standing by the little station lifted his hat and shouted, ' Vive la Commune ! ' This unknown man made Louise pull herself together. ' I felt something very like a promise to remain worthy of those words,' she wrote, profoundly moved.

110 SEVEN WOMEN AGAINST THE WORLD

She spent eight long years in New Caledonia. She studied botany; she taught the children of the other prisoners; she read whenever she found a scrap of paper with print on it; she was utterly lonely. But she was not without hope. News reached the colony of Blanqui's London Manifesto of 1874, in which he advocated the Class War; of the Congress of Workers which met in Marseilles in 1879. The organization of the workers was progressing; the fact that they were becoming more articulate was reflected in the growing number of socialist newspapers in France: *La Bataille, Le Prolétaire, Cri du Peuple, L'Égalité.*

It is astonishing how quickly Louise readjusted herself to life after her return to France from New Caledonia. After all, she was now a woman of over fifty, the penal colony had been a terrible experience, and shortly after she came home Marie Ferré died. Her friend's death was a great shock to her. Nothing, however, could affect Louise's vitality, her singleness of purpose, but her attitude towards the social revolution had undergone a change. Years at the colony had instilled into her a loathing of authority of any kind, and she was now attracted by the doctrines of anarchists like Michel Bakunin or Kropotkin.

She plunged again into political activities, travelling all over France to hold meetings and to organize the workers. She was a brilliant speaker, quick at repartee, and her great knowledge impressed even her enemies. She was a formidable opponent, a woman without fear, chiefly because she valued her own life so little, and she made the French authorities extremely uncomfortable. They began to watch her carefully very soon after her return from New Caledonia; she was sent to prison for two weeks in 1882 for taking part in a demonstration held to commemorate the eighty-second anniversary of Blanqui's birth.

LOUISE MICHEL

In 1883, when unemployment was increasing in France, Louise joined a procession of hunger marchers in Paris. During this huge demonstration a number of bakery shops were broken into, the bread was stolen, and distributed among the marching crowd. When it was known that Louise Michel had been among the marchers, the police immediately suspected her. Finally she was brought to trial for inciting the crowd to rob the bakeries. An example was made of her case, and she was sentenced to six years' imprisonment.

The French Government can certainly not look back with pride on the treatment given this woman. If she had actually incited the crowd to break into the bakery shops she would have admitted it proudly at her trial : she herself declared that the police had sent *agents provocateurs* to do so. But even had she been responsible, six years' imprisonment seems a very harsh sentence.

Her attitude at her trial probably increased the Court's prejudice against her, for she was so obviously disrespectful of property as such. She defended the unemployed workers of Paris by saying that as they were giving no work, they were justified in taking bread if they were hungry. And her manner expressed the same contempt for her judges which is implied in Anatole France's remark about the fairness of a judicial system which gives exactly the same punishment for both the rich and the poor if they steal a loaf of bread.

Louise spent the first part of her sentence at the women's prison at Saint Lazare, and she was then transferred to the Central Prison at Clairmont. She had become a legend in France, and in both prisons she was respectfully called ' Madame la Pétroleuse,' for her fellow-prisoners were convinced that she had set fire to many buildings in Paris during the Commune. She made dresses for the other prisoners—despite her

112 SEVEN WOMEN AGAINST THE WORLD

masculine characteristics she was an expert seamstress; she taught the illiterates among them ; she read aloud to them,

In both prisons, furthermore, she came into contact with prostitutes. This was a phase of society she had never studied before, and, idealist that she was, she firmly believed that the new order would remove this evil with every other one.

In 1884 a cholera epidemic broke out in Paris. Louise's anxiety about her mother prompted her to ask a favour of the prison authorities for the first time in her life ; she asked to be allowed to go to Paris, where she could, at least, be near Madame Michel. Her request was granted, and she was sent back to Saint Lazare, where her mother could come to see her. The old woman was, however, taken ill and died early in 1885. Louise felt that, as far as her private interests were concerned, life was over for her. Now ' she had nothing left but the Revolution,' and personally, ' the future was dead for her, she did not want to go on living except in the past.'

Her profound depression at this time is reflected in the dedication in her *Memoirs*, completed some years later. She wrote :

' To MYRIAM

Myriam they were both called :

My mother

My friend.

I send forth my book to their graves.

I wish my life would spend itself quickly so that I could join them.

And now, if by chance, my work does any good, no one should be grateful to me, for I worked merely to numb my grief.

The great enemy is near me. Having nothing to hope, and nothing to fear, I hurry towards the goal, like those who fling away their drinking cups with the dregs in them.'

LOUISE MICHEL 113

The prison governor at Saint Lazare was moved to pity for this elderly woman. He recommended that she be pardoned with other prisoners on the 14th of July 1885. She had seemed so broken after her mother's death that he did not think she could be a danger to the State again. The kindly man was pleased when his request for her pardon was granted, and he sent for her to break the good news to her. She was extremely polite, but she refused this pardon in no uncertain terms. 'I wish to accept no favours whatsoever from the men who are governing our country at present,' she told him firmly, and returned to her cell.

'Thank you,' she wrote to Lissagaray at this time, 'I see that you have understood that I could not, without dishonour, have accepted a pardon to which I had no more right than the others.

'Everything or nothing.

'I don't want them to pay me with a pardon for my mother's dead body. Thank the friends who warned me in time that this pardon was coming.'

Her refusal to accept this pardon renewed the authorities' suspicions of her. Besides, the working classes of France were slowly recovering from the defeat of the Commune, and the Government was nervous. The Second International was founded in 1889, and Socialists were actively organizing in France. Constans, then French Minister of the Interior, was particularly frightened of this working-class movement, and for some reason Louise Michel became his *bête noir*. He was preparing for the time when she would be released from prison.

When she left Saint Lazare, Louise resumed her political work at once. Unlike most active people who have been in prison for a long time, she did not seem to need a period of readjustment before she could resume a free life. One feels that she could

8

114 SEVEN WOMEN AGAINST THE WORLD

have gone directly from a solitary prison cell to a crowded Socialist or Anarchist meeting and spoken to a crowd with her usual vigour.

Almost immediately after her dismissal from Saint Lazare she was talking before an audience of over two thousand men and women in the Salle Franklin at Havre. In the middle of her lecture she was suddenly shot at by a man named Pierre Lucas, who was obviously very drunk. It has never been made clear who had incited him, but it was quite obvious that he was acting for some one else. Louise, at any rate, was convinced of this, and she spent a great deal of time defending him, caring for his distracted wife, and assuring the judges that he was merely weak and not really wicked. ' Above all,' she said to Labbé, her surgeon at the Beaujou hospital, after she had reminded him that she was a fighter and not a woman, ' above all, assure the judges that the wound itself is nothing, merely a scratch.'

Louise recovered from this wound in her ear, and the next year, 1890, when she was sixty years old, she joined the strikers in the Vienne District. She was with the strikers, or led them, wherever factories were attacked ; whether strike-breakers were pursued or beaten by the strikers. Wherever the movement was strongest, Louise was with the men. Finally she was arrested and taken to Lyons.

Here she had the most dastardly experience of her entire career. She had always believed that the warders were unenlightened men, or they would not assist the authorities, but she never held them responsible for any suffering, any humilation they inflicted on her. Constans knew this, and the warder at the Lyons prison was instructed to make her drunk before the trial. He came into her cell smiling good-naturedly, and offered her some weak wine with water. She accepted, not suspecting the man, and not realizing that the drink he gave her was very strong.

LOUISE MICHEL

When she was brought into the Court, her walk was uncertain, her speech, normally so clear and concise, was incoherent. She was dismissed as 'irresponsible,' and the court dared to ridicule a woman of her age, dignity and record of courage for being drunk. When Louise left Havre, still not realizing exactly what had happened, and thinking she must have been taken suddenly ill, she went back to Paris to her tiny flat. Fortunately her friends had found out that Constans planned to have her certified and sent to an insane asylum. The trick in the Havre prison was merely to be the first step in this plan.

By these means Louise had finally been temporarily defeated. She and her friend Charlotte Vauvelle left France and came to London. She lived in London for five years, though she went often to Paris to address meetings. She devoted her energies to collecting money for revolutions which were expected to break out in Belgium and Italy and other European countries.

When she was in England she went to the Fabian Society, she attended meetings of an anarchist club, the Autonomy, which met in Windmill Street, she followed with avid interest revolutionary events all over Europe, especially in Russia.

She lived with Charlotte Vauvelle, Monsieur Vauvelle, her aged father, and her brother. Part of the time they were in a cottage at East Dulwich. To strangers, Louise Michel may have seemed like an ordinary crank, who was madly attached to animals. She picked up stray cats and dogs, and her home was full of birds as well. But when she began to talk, when one studied that fine ugly face more closely, something of what she had been through in her long and eventful life was communicated to the listener.

Charles Malato, who visited her in London, was struck by her faith in the future, by her belief that the

116 SEVEN WOMEN AGAINST THE WORLD

working classes must eventually win in the struggle. ' She had the same faith in the future,' he wrote, ' the same serene impassiveness. She was a strange figure, who did not seem to belong to our own prosaic age, but to the past or to the future. She went through life—that life full of conflicts, deportations, imprisonment, persecution, and continuous apostleship—always enveloped in a black dress, which was like a flag of despair and of revolt . . . '

In 1896 Louise Michel returned to France, where she set forth on a most strenuous lecture tour, speaking on revolutionary developments in Russia. For the next eight years she continued to hold meetings wherever and whenever she was asked to do so, and her powers as a public speaker were not impaired by her age. Her vitality was so great that men, years younger than herself, were often exhausted when they travelled with her.

She worked until the end. She was taken ill at Troyes, where she had been speaking, and she died on January 10, 1905.

She died content, feeling that the cause for which she had given her entire life was soon to win. The subject of her last lecture was ' Antimilitarism and the Russian Revolution.' Her last thoughts were about Russia, this country she had never seen, and which, she was convinced, would realize the aims for which her friends had died after the defeat of the Commune. In one of her last conversations with Ernest Girault, with whom she was travelling, she said to him, happy that she had never lost her faith : ' Watch developments in Russia . . . You will see that in the country of Gorki and Kropotkin tremendous events will occur. I see a revolution rising and growing which will remove the Tsar . . . and what will be most surprising will be the fact that in Moscow, in Petersburg, in Cronstadt, in Sebastopol, the soldiers will side with the people.'

LOUISE MICHEL

She died as consciously, as courageously, as she had lived, convinced that the working classes of the world would soon appreciate that their ' deliverance from oppression would not come by itself ' ; that they would soon realize that ' they must take this freedom by force, instead of begging for it.'

V

VERA FIGNER (1852–   )

SOME one once said that Russia, whose social transition
has been so abrupt, is not like a man maturing gradually and normally, but like a giant awakening. Vera
Nicolajevna Figner was active at that period in Russia's
history when this giant was stirring for the first time ;
she herself contributed actively to his ultimate awakening.

She was born in Kasan on June 24, 1852, and she
became one of those early Russian Revolutionaries
who were popularly known throughout Europe as the
' Nihilists.' In the 'seventies these men and women,
most of them young and from the educated classes,
carried out a series of terrorist acts, which culminated,
in 1881, in the assassination of Tsar Alexander II.
These revolutionaries believed that the despotism
dominating their country could be shaken only by
the assassination of individuals responsible for the
medieval tyranny which prevailed in Russia.

Vera Figner and her friends were the pioneers of
Russia's social revolution. Before their time no effective organized revolt had occurred in Russia. Sporadic
rebellions, such as that planned by the ' Decabrists '
—the men of December—in December 1825 had
failed, and the liberal teachings of certain courageous
intellectuals, such as Dostojewski, in the 'forties, or
Alexander Herzen, in the 'fifties, had helped to educate
the Russian middle classes, but had no concrete or
lasting results.

Looking back, it is not difficult to understand why
ardent believers in human liberties like Vera Figner
made and used bombs. In Western countries, with

120 SEVEN WOMEN AGAINST THE WORLD

growing industrial populations, propagandistic methods of educating the masses and influencing the electorate were practical and possible. In Russia, on the other hand, a preponderantly agricultural country, where industry did not develop until relatively late in the century, and where the peasantry was largely illiterate, reform would have been a hopeless task.

Any efforts to bring about a change in the social structure by means of a gradual process of evolution must have seemed particularly futile to impatient young humanitarians, who were constantly aware of the terrible oppression and social injustices in Russia, where the whim of the Tsar could affect the lives of millions.

How quickly, historically speaking, conditions in Russia have changed is shown by the fact that Vera Figner, who is to-day living in Soviet Russia, was born nine years before serfdom was abolished in her country. The serfs were freed in 1861, at a time when revolutionaries in other countries were already preparing for a class war, where the doctrines of Marx were spreading rapidly. Vera Figner's contemporaries in other countries could remember when the working classes were still more bitterly oppressed, when the struggle for universal suffrage was being waged.

Vera Figner, on the other hand, knew a time when, in Russia, men and women were slaves. The thought that they might fight for a fairer distribution of wealth had not yet occurred to the few serfs who may have hoped vaguely that their grandchildren might be taught to read and write ; for these serfs were like animals in that they did not own their own bodies. Serfdom reflects how many generations, from the point of view of human progress, Russia lagged behind other countries. This fact should be borne in mind when the violent methods of these early Russian Revolutionaries is considered. The backwardness of their country must have filled them with an uncon-

VERA FIGNER

trollable desire to fight with any weapons for the human rights of their fellow-countrymen.

Even with the help of a great many photographs it is difficult to describe Vera Figner's appearance. The features of her narrow face are perfectly proportioned ; her small mouth gentle but firm ; her slender nose very sensitive ; and her dark penetrating eyes are sad, but by no means without a look of hope and confidence. The most remarkable thing about her recent photographs is the compactness, the determination still retained in her face. Evelyn Sharp, who saw Vera Figner in Moscow over ten years ago, writes :

' That she was composed and quiet in voice and manner, and quite unlike what one might expect a woman to be who had attempted to assassinate a Tsar, was not surprising, because the slightest experience of revolutionists is enough to lead one to expect this kind of outward calm of those who string themselves up to do deeds entirely at variance with their inner nature for the sake of some cause. But what did seem astonishing was that she looked so young, her hair still only slightly grey and her eyes as bright as those of a young girl, though I was told that she was then seventy-two. It was hardly credible that she had passed twenty years in solitary confinement in a Russian fortress, an experience so terrible that, she told me, all her companions who were sentenced at the same time had either died or lost their reason. . . . The picture I carried away of this wonderful old rebel woman is unforgettable, as is the impression of concentrated force and spiritual reticence that she seemed to shed round her.'

Vera Figner's life, like that of Louise Michel, is divided into two distinct periods : one of which was completely absorbed by her political activities, while during the other she remained outside the conflict. Vera Figner, however, in contrast to Louise Michel,

122 SEVEN WOMEN AGAINST THE WORLD

spent her early years as an active revolutionary. During the second part of her life she was forced to be completely passive: for twenty years she was imprisoned in the most terrible Tsarist fortress-prison, the Schluesselburg, where for many years she was not allowed to correspond with her own family, and where she was cut off entirely from news of the outside world. She could not, even at a distance, observe the social developments of her country.

Her childhood was like that of other young Russian aristocrats of her generation. Her father, Nicolai Alexandrovitch Figner, a government forester, was stationed at Kasan. Vera was the eldest of six children, four girls and two boys. Vera's mother, Jekaterina Christoforovna Figner, so Vera writes in her *Memoirs*, was 'gentle and good,' but obviously awed by her husband, who had a violent temper and was a severe disciplinarian. The children lived according to the strictest rules: They had to get up and go to bed at a certain time, and their father punished them severely if they were a minute late. At table they were not permitted to speak; their food and their clothing were strictly supervised. Their father trained them to stand extreme cold and extreme heat; no weakness of any kind was tolerated. They were never allowed to complain.

Vera Figner was nevertheless deeply attached to her mother. Even as a very young girl she realized that Jekatarina Christoforovna could not have made their childhood happier. She was too weak to oppose her husband; she was made quite as miserable as were her children by his relentless severity. Vera Figner admits, however, that when she was a child her old nurse was the only mature person who ever showed her or her brothers and sisters any real understanding or affection.

' There was one bright spot in this deadly barracks atmosphere,' she wrote many decades later, ' there was

one comfort and one joy : our old nurse. No one else
in our home had the slightest understanding for children or for children's needs. Childish weaknesses were
never tolerated ; we were surrounded by cruelty and
hardness. Only in Nurse's room, which my father
never entered, only when we were with her, did we
feel that we could be ourselves ; with her we felt
like human beings, like children and like masters ;
above all, however, we felt like spoiled children. Her
room was our sanctuary ; here we could win back our
self-respect after we had been hurt or humiliated.
Here we could divulge our childish sorrows, here we
found sympathy and tenderness.'

The governesses who came to the Figner home
carried out Nicolai Alexandrowitch's wishes conscien-
tiously. Vera Figner remembers that she was awakened
one night, when her governess, a lighted candle in
one hand, was stretching the little girl's hand : that
day she had not been able to reach an octave on the
piano, and the governess, greatly concerned, was trying
to remedy this shortcoming.

Occasionally the children were taken to visit
elderly relatives who lived on neighbouring estates,
but as a rule they lived a completely isolated life.
No outside influences disturbed the regular routine
of the forester's home. This seclusion caused his
children to be particularly devoted to each other ;
they rarely saw any other boys or girls of their own age.
Two of Vera's sisters, Lydia and Eugenie, were later
both banished to Siberia for their political activities.
Her youngest sister, Olga, was not herself involved
as a revolutionary, but she went to Siberia with her
husband, a doctor, who lived in exile for many years.
Vera's brothers were not political ; one of them was a
well-known opera singer, the other a mining engineer,
but the loyalty both of them felt for their sisters
never wavered despite their political differences.

When Vera Figner was eleven years old she was

124 SEVEN WOMEN AGAINST THE WORLD

sent to the Kasan Institute, a girls' school not unlike the famous Smolny Institute, where the daughters of Russian aristocrats were educated. Life at a convent could not have been more narrow than it was at the Kasan Institute. The pupils never met strangers, least of all young people of their own age. Only twice during the year were they taken for a walk outside the Institute grounds ; during the rest of the terms they lived inside the high walls which surrounded the school buildings. They were obliged to spend the summer before their last term at the Institute, as it was feared by the authorities that a lack of discipline in their homes might be bad for the pupils before their final and difficult months at the school.

Vera's fellow-students probably met other young people in their own homes, but she was now cut off from the outside world more rigorously than she had been as a child. Her early life seems like a preparation for that terrible seclusion she was to know for so many years at Schluesselburg. She records that, incredible as this seems, as a young girl she only met two strangers. During one summer holiday, when she was at home, two students from the Kasan University came to see her father, and she never forgot them, as it was such a tremendous event to see any one not belonging to her family or the school at Kasan.

Life at the Kasan Institute consisted chiefly of rules and regulations, of lessons learned by heart ; there was little real education. And one dancing lesson a week was the only physical training provided for the girls, apart from slow proper walks in the walled-in gardens. Reading was not encouraged, and only once during the six years she spent there does Vera Figner remember receiving a book from the Institute library.

As Vera liked reading better than she did anything else, she was confined to the books her schoolfellows, who had relatives at Kasan, borrowed from them and smuggled into the school. Most of these books were popular novels, and none of them made much impression on her. Lights were put out early, and in order to read late Vera Figner often knelt before the icon in the corner of the large room in which the girls slept. She would hold her book up to the flickering candle before the holy picture, and hide it quickly, pretending that she was praying, when the mistress came in to inspect the dormitory.

There was nothing to stimulate Vera Figner's active mind at the Kasan Institute, but when she left it in 1869 she already hoped, if somewhat vaguely, that she might continue her studies, or perhaps go to a university, if she could make her parents consent to such a plan. Reactionary as Tsarist Russia was in other ways, the general attitude towards the education of women was not quite as conservative as it was in other countries. Among some educated people, as early as the late 'sixties, it was not considered entirely wild or fantastic for women to attend a university, and one Russian woman, Suslowa, had already qualified as a physician and a surgeon at the University of Zürich.

When Vera Figner returned to her home from Kasan she soon realized that her father had not mellowed in the least. True, her mother now took more interest in her, giving her modern books and periodicals, but life was as dull and uninspiring as it had been when she was younger. For the first time in her life, however, Vera had an opportunity of associating with thinking and intelligent people ; she frequently saw her mother's brother and his wife, her aunt and uncle Kuprijanov.

The Kuprijanovs and their friends, whom Vera met, were by no means Socialists or Republicans. She never heard them mention Fourier, Saint-Simon, or the other forerunners of modern Socialism, and it

126 SEVEN WOMEN AGAINST THE WORLD

is probable that they never discussed Marx, though his doctrines were already a popular topic of conversation among the intellectuals, and his *Capital* was published in Russia a few years later in 1873.

As Vera Figner herself says, she was at this time completely ignorant of those Socialist theories which were later to occupy her entire life. She had not the slightest conception of the social upheavals which were occurring outside Russia, nor did she understand conditions in her own country. She remembers that she still confused the name of Laplace with that of Lassalle.

There is no question, however, that her uncle Kuprijanov began her real education. He was what was then called a ' Liberal-Democrat,' a man without social or religious prejudices, who was not horrified to discover that his niece's views on religion were not orthodox. On the contrary, he encouraged her obvious interest in science : he gave her Darwin and Lyell to read. Kuprijanov was a great admirer of the economic doctrines of Tschernyshevsky, but it is doubtful whether her uncle thought Vera mature enough to give her copies of this economist's periodical *Sovremjennik*, the *Contemporary*. Vera Figner's uncle did not fully appreciate the indomitable will to learn which was hidden behind her quiet and respectful manner.

Vera Figner has always remained deeply grateful to this uncle who ' first awakened in her the wish to find some useful activity.' As yet she had no definite interest in social or political problems, but he did teach her a utilitarian philosophy—' the greatest good to the greatest number '—and he prompted her to contemplate the useless lives led by the majority of the leisured class and wealthy aristocracy to which she belonged.

When one remembers that three years later she had already resolved to dedicate her life to

VERA FIGNER 127

Socialism, it is surprising that at this period she was still hoping confusedly merely to alleviate the sufferings of mankind. It had not yet occurred to her to believe that the whole system in Russia was wrong, that no lasting good could be accomplished by a temporary relief of the human misery which prevailed.

'The vague conception,' she declared at her trial in 1884, 'that I belonged to an educated minority caused me to consider the duties of a woman born with my advantages towards the uneducated masses, who merely exist from day to day, who are oppressed by heavy physical labour, and who have no share in what we usually call ' the benefits of civilization.' A comparison of my own situation with that of so many other human beings, first made me realize that my aim in life must be to help these fellow-creatures.'

With this aim in view, medicine was, of course, the most obvious profession Vera Figner could have chosen. She therefore determined to become a physician ; she did not care whether she went to the University of Kasan, to St. Petersburg, or abroad. Her parents opposed this plan more stubbornly than she had anticipated ; they suddenly wondered whether, by cutting her off from the companionship of young people of her own age, they themselves had not been to blame for her unusual seriousness, her one-sided intellectual interests.

So they took her to Kasan, where she was plunged from complete seclusion into a whirl of social gaieties. Naturally, she was shy and unsure of herself, and the first large ball she attended was a most unpleasant experience. She was so unhappy that she ' almost wept.'

The visit in Kasan had very important consequences for Vera Figner. She had stayed in the home of some friends of her parents, and the eldest son of this family, Alexei Viktorovitch Filipov, a young judge, indirectly helped her to leave home and go to a

128 SEVEN WOMEN AGAINST THE WORLD

university. Soon after she left Kasan he arranged to be transferred as an examining magistrate to a district near the Figner's home. He then saw Vera Figner often, and as he believed in a higher education for women, he was enthusiastic about her plans to study medicine. She married Filipov on October 16, 1870.

Shortly afterwards her father died, and her mother went to live in Kasan with her younger brothers and sisters. Vera Figner and her husband continued to live in the country, but she planned to go to some university in Switzerland as soon as she could afford it. She hated the laws in force in Russia, and as a result she urged her husband to give up the legal profession. She finally persuaded him to resign from his post and to study medicine with her. She herself devoted the eighteen months before they went to Zürich to perfecting her German and to the study of algebra and geometry.

Vera Figner was a very serious and determined young woman when, at the age of nineteen, she entered the University of Zürich with her husband and her sister Lydia, who had decided to join the Filipovs. At first Vera worked so hard that she made few friends, but within a few months she knew many of the other women students in Zürich, and she became interested in subjects not included in her medical course.

From Russian refugees Vera Figner learned more about her own country than she had known at home ; her conceptions about politics were growing less vague. She heard about the activities of the International Association of Working Men ; she was asked to contribute funds for the Communarde victims of the Paris Commune, for the victims of the Spanish Revolution. She studied the theories of Socialism, the history of social oppression, especially in Russia.

Vera Figner never did anything half-heartedly. Soon she joined a study circle of twelve members—all young Russian women students—who were making

VERA FIGNER

a world survey of Socialism. The work they planned for their study circle is so doctrinaire that one might have thought them merely a group of theoretical young enthusiasts. Actually, however, all of them later became active revolutionaries, who paid the price of imprisonment, exile, or death for their belief. Their programme, drafted in 1872, is worth quoting, as it is so like the programmes of students of our own time :

(1) To study Socialist teachings from Thomas More to the present day ; above all, the theories of Fourier, Saint-Simon, Cabet, Louis Blanc, Proudhon, Lassalle.

(2) To study political economy.

(3) To study the history of social upheavals and revolutions.

(4) To study labour problems and the labour movements in Western countries (History of English Trades Unions, International Working Men's Association, General German Workers' Association).

By the early summer of 1873 the Russian Government had been informed of the subversive attitude of the group of women students to which Vera Figner belonged. At the time, some people thought it ridiculous that the Tsar of All the Russians should have been seriously disturbed by the theoretical arguments of these young women, but history later showed that the Tsarist régime's anxiety was fully justified. At any rate, the Tsar issued a decree demanding that these women students leave Zürich at once. If they did not do so, so the decree stipulated, they would never be accepted for a State examination in Russia. For Vera Figner this meant that if she did not leave she would not be allowed to practise medicine in Russia.

The tactlessness and foolishness of the Tsar's government was reflected in one passage of this communication, which gave as one reason for the decree that these students were devoting much of their time

130 SEVEN WOMEN AGAINST THE WORLD

to ' free love.' These serious-minded young women were concerned with broader political issues. They gave little thought to the fact that they were also pioneers in the education of women, but this accusation angered them profoundly and roused their feminist instincts. Vera Figner always remembered this unnecessary insult.

A few of her fellow-students returned to Russia to continue their studies and to begin their secret political activities. Vera's sister Lydia, and some of the others, decided to spend the next term at the University of Paris, and Vera herself, with the Ljubatevitch sisters and Kaminskaja, went to the University of Bern.

Vera Figner had changed completely while she was in Zürich, or perhaps these surroundings, where she could exchange and express her own ideas, had merely stimulated and matured the potentialities that were always in her. Her husband was not pleased with her new outlook, and he disapproved of her Socialist friends. By nature conservative, her ardent defence of extreme political doctrines turned him, for the time being, into a reactionary. They had far less in common than they had before they came abroad, and when she went to Bern he did not join her. He returned to Russia and resumed his legal career.

The fact that Vera Figner and Filipov parted— they were later divorced—is symptomatic of her growing independence. Her entire attitude towards life had altered during this one short year. The study of medicine, which had been her one objective, now seemed relatively unimportant.

' What had been her aim was now merely the means to an end. The activities of a physician, an agriculturist, a technician had become meaningless ; they seemed nothing but welfare work, a palliative. She and her friends did not want to cure only the symptoms of the disease ; instead, they wanted to

VERA FIGNER
131

uproot and remove its causes. They now realized that even if they could treat the people with medicines, pills, or mixtures, the most they could ever do was to bring about a temporary improvement in their condition. The diseases themselves would not be removed or lessened, because the fundamental condition of the masses—their unfavourable living, food, and clothing conditions—would remain unchanged. The professional aim, which had seemed to these young students so idealistic and so splendid, had been lowered in their eyes into a mere craft—and a useless one at that.'

Despite her disillusionment about medicine, it obviously never occurred to Vera Figner to give up her studies. Probably she realized, if somewhat unconsciously, that to become really effective politically she must have another profession as well. At any rate, she arranged to go to Bern.

The summer before she matriculated at Bern, Vera Figner spent her holidays at the Neuenberger See with her sister Lydia, who had already joined a secret revolutionary organization which had begun to work in Russia. The original statutes of this organization—including at the beginning twelve young women, all of them students, some of whom were already working in Russia—were based on those of the International Association of Working Men, a purely Western European association. In their enthusiasm Lydia and her associates at first forgot how radically conditions in Russia differed from those in other, more liberal, and more highly industrialized countries. Just as to-day, Russian Communists, who are convinced that Communism will eventually conquer everywhere, make the mistake of trying to impose Russian Communism on Western Europe, where conditions are so unlike those prevailing in Russia.

These early Russian revolutionaries were thinking in terms of collectivism : every individual must work

132 SEVEN WOMEN AGAINST THE WORLD

according to his ability ; every individual must be given the material goods he needs. Actually, of course, in Russia, where modern industry was only just beginning to develop, and where a despotism, as absolute as that which existed in France before the French Revolution, still reigned, the ground had not been prepared for nineteenth-century Socialism. The first task of these revolutionaries, as they soon realized, was to try to undermine the Tsarist government.

One lovely evening, when Vera and her sister were walking by the shores of the Lake, Lydia solemnly asked her whether she was determined to devote her life to the social revolution. Lydia read the statutes of the new organization to her. Vera said that she was ready to give her life, if necessary, to this cause. She was not gradually drawn into revolutionary activities, as were so many other fighters for social justice. On the contrary, she took her pledge in the abstract, for an idea, while she was miles away from the country where she agreed to join the conflict. She never broke this promise she had given her sister. She was then only twenty-one years old.

While Vera Figner was a student in Bern she was closely in touch with the illegal activities of her own and other groups in Russia. She saw many of the Socialists living in exile abroad, and she was in a position to help many of them financially. She also became interested in an *emigré* newspaper, *Rabotnik* (*The Workmen*) which was published outside of Russia.

The organization to which Vera Figner belonged now included twenty-five members who were busily engaged in Socialist propaganda in Russia. They agreed to help the workers in case of strikes or sporadic revolts, but they still believed that the masses could be educated to Socialism by entirely peaceful means ; they aimed to build up a democratic association of the workers. These young revolutionaries temporarily

VERA FIGNER 133

gave up their own intellectual interests and worked in factories side by side with the men and women whom they wanted to educate. Some of them went into Moscow industries ; others learned weaving and were employed in the growing weaving industry at Ivanovo-Vasnessensk ; while others worked in the sugar plants at Kiev.

In the autumn of 1875 the police discovered this organization and many of its most efficient members, including Lydia Figner, who had returned to Russia some time before, were arrested. They were later tried in the famous ' Trial of the Fifty,' and most of them were banished to Siberia.

The members of the organization who had not been caught wrote at once to Vera Figner, and the other members who were abroad, urging them to come back to Russia at once. In six months she was to have taken her medical degree ; if she left Bern now she would never become a qualified surgeon and physician. She might become a nurse or a midwife, for these examinations would be open to her in Russia, but she could never practise medicine. Her mother, to whom she was devoted, would be bitterly disappointed. Vera Figner's conflict, however, was brief. Young as she was, she had fully realized that under the circumstances no compromise was possible. She returned to Russia.

She had given up everything for the principles in which she believed. When she was in Moscow she did not go to the prison on the visitor's day to see her sister Lydia, for this would have attracted the authorities' attention to her and hampered the task before her. This young and attractive woman of twenty-three had already decided that ' the work before her would consume so much of her intellectual and moral energy that she must exclude all personal elements from her life.' Some years later, when she joined the Narodnaya Volya Party, the Party of The *People's*

134 SEVEN WOMEN AGAINST THE WORLD

Will, this resolve was crystallized into a more definite decision. With the other members of the Party she adhered to the revolutionary catechism and promised that ' she would devote all her mental and spiritual powers to the revolution, for the sake of which she would sacrifice all ties of family, all other sympathies ; she would give up love and friendship.'

It is a curious fact that though Vera Figner had been obsessed for almost three years with the idea of the social revolution, though she had already decided to sacrifice everything to it, she had never, before she returned to Russia in 1876, been an active participant in the struggle. She had never been in contact with reality, with everyday problems, with the actual difficulties of spreading revolutionary doctrines in a despotic country. She experienced many disappointments : the group to which she belonged had been thoroughly disorganized by the police ; many of the members had lost their heads ; they were in constant danger from spies and informers.

This trying period was made easier for her by Anton Taksis, a follower of Lavrov. He helped her to realize that the failure of their organization was due chiefly to the inexperience of its members, and he taught her that in any social conflict, enthusiasm, though necessary, is not as important as an ability for hard routine work. He encouraged her to go to the country and to try to educate the peasants.

Before she left Moscow, Vera Figner had joined the new revolutionary organization, including at first about 160 members, which was founded by Mark Andrejevitch Nathanson late in 1876. This group, called *Land and Liberty*, after an organization which had existed in the 'sixties, admitted that industry was not yet sufficiently developed in Russia to make it worth while for the members to concentrate their efforts on the emancipation of industrial labour. The ultimate aim of *Land and Liberty* was to wrest the

VERA FIGNER

land from the big landowners and to give it to the Russian people. It was resolved, furthermore, to spread Socialist doctrines among all classes of society; among the army and navy, the civil administration, the bourgeoisie, and, above all, among the peasantry. Huge mass demonstrations were advocated as a means of awakening public opinion.

Vera Figner witnessed the first of these ill-fated demonstrations in St Petersburg, on December 6, 1876. Plechanov, one of the original members of *Land and Liberty*, made a courageous speech, after which a young workman, Jakob Potapov, unfurled a red flag. He was arrested. Vera and her sister Eugenie were so inexperienced that they did not hurry as they left the demonstration. Instead they stayed together and walked calmly down the broad Nevski-Prospekt where any one could see them. A fellow-revolutionary, whom Vera and her sister had asked to come home with them for lunch, was arrested, and they escaped only by jumping into a passing cab while the police were busy with him.

After this demonstration, some of the members of *Land and Liberty* remained in St. Petersburg, while others, including Vera Figner and her sister Eugenie, went to country districts. They first went to Samara and later to Semstvo, in Saratov, where Vera Figner was employed as a matron in a hospital. Her sister founded a free school; at the time, for a population of 30,000 souls, there was not a single free school in the town.

The illiteracy was so great in this district, the living standards so low, that Vera Figner realized almost from the beginning how hopeless was her task. Human beings, who could not read or write, could not be expected to be receptive to Socialist doctrines. For two years Vera and her sister tried to educate the peasants by reading aloud to them, by talking to them, by encouraging them to think, by

136 SEVEN WOMEN AGAINST THE WORLD

raising their level of intelligence. The two young women themselves lived in the utmost simplicity. They rarely had meat, and never ate white bread. They spent only ten or twelve roubles a month of Vera's salary of twenty-five roubles. The rest was distributed among the poor.

It was conspicuous for women, obviously well-born and well educated, to spend so much time with illiterate people, and, above all, to treat them as equals, and some of the gentry in the town, especially the priest, soon became suspicious of Vera and her sister. The priest spread the rumour that they were advocating subversive teachings. He did so merely to get rid of them, for he did not know that their sister Lydia was in Siberia. Though Vera's papers were quite in order, she could not afford to have the police delve into her past record, and so, in 1879, she and Eugenie, both of them disillusioned about the prospects of peaceful propaganda, returned to St. Petersburg.

Events outside their confined life in Semstvo bore out their growing conviction that only by terroristic acts could the terroristic methods of the Government be combated. During the first decade of the reign of Alexander II he had introduced a number of reforms. Serfdom was abolished, and the old despotic tribunals were replaced by courts more like those in Western Europe. Later, however, the Tsar discontinued his policy of reform, and a period of intense reaction set in. From early in 1878 until the summer of the following year, when Vera Figner left Semstvo, eighteen political prisoners were executed, and many more were imprisoned or exiled to Siberia.

Before she left Semstvo, Alexander Solojov, who later made an unsuccessful attempt to assassinate the Tsar, came to see her, and strengthened her belief in violence as the only practical method. When she returned to St. Petersburg she became a founder-member of the *Peoples' Will*, the Narodnaya Volya

VERA FIGNER

Party. It has often been said that the Terror was the chief aim of this Party, but this was not the case. The Terror was adopted as a measure of ridding the country of its despotic influences, such as General Mezentsor, the head of the political police, who was later assassinated, and of intimidating the entire administration. If, for instance, the Narodnaya Volya heard that political exiles were being badly treated in Siberia, a member went to the head of the Prison Inspection Department in St. Petersburg and killed him, if necessary, to attract the country's attention to the state of affairs.

The terrorist methods adopted by the Narodnaya Volya were so sensational, that the members of the Party were often considered destructive anarchists. This conception is entirely untrue. They were fighting for liberty, but never for lawlessness ; many of them were not even thinking in terms of a Socialist Russia of the future. In her trial Vera Figner herself declared that she had fought all her life for a destruction of the despotic régime. Then she went on to say : ' Whether our programme will eventually provide for a Republic or a constitutional monarchy does not seem to me to be of any practical importance.'

Later generations have often overlooked this point of view, and it is sometimes forgotten that the Narodnaya Volya had very definite plans for taking over the Government when the Tsar and his régime had been removed. At first a purely democratic programme was planned, and a dictatorship of the Party as such was not contemplated. A provisional government was to govern the country until a general election had been held and a constitutional assembly had been called together. Later, in a memorandum, ' Preparations of the Party,' the question was raised as to whether it would not be more expedient for the Party itself to take over power. Even then, however, the Party did not intend to force its programme on the constitutional

138 SEVEN WOMEN AGAINST THE WORLD

assembly ; instead, peaceful propaganda was to be the means of educating the masses to the Party's point of view.

At the time, when one attempt at assassination followed another, the majority of Liberals in Russia gave the Narodnaya Volya their moral support ; every successful assassination was welcomed by the enlightened bourgeoisie with hushed applause. Their timidity can easily be understood, but it is one of the injustices of history that with notable exceptions, such as Bardovski, the lawyer who defended many of the revolutionaries, and lost his mind when he himself was arrested, Liberals in Russia in the 'seventies, 'eighties, and even later, sat back while young women like Vera Figner risked their lives and their freedom, or gave them, for the sake of a free Russia. Perhaps had the liberal-minded element of the population contributed more actively to the abolition of the cruel and despotic Tsarist régime, the extremists in Russian politics would not have been victorious in the end. As the revolutionaries made all the sacrifices history would have been unusually ironical had she given the victory to the more moderate parties.

Vera Figner began her active illegal life as a member of the Narodnaya Volya late in 1879. She and one of her associates, Kvatovski, took a house in Lenoi, a suburb of St. Petersburg. Their home became the central headquarters of the group of Narodnaya Volya members who were planning the assassination of the Tsar.

It was decided to ' execute ' him when he returned from the Crimea after his summer holiday. Dynamite was to be laid along the three railway routes he might choose on his return to St. Petersburg : the route Moscow-Kursk, Losovaja-Sevastopol, or Odessa.

Vera Figner herself was sent to Odessa with the necessary explosive. It was agreed that the mine could best be laid under the railway lines by a fellow-

VERA FIGNER   139

conspirator who was to be disguised as a flagman near the station.

Dressed as a member of the landed gentry (to which, of course, she belonged by birth) Vera went to see the Governor of Odessa. She told him that one of the caretakers on her estate was ill with tuberculosis, that the man needed a change of air, and that she had come to see whether the railway could give him a post as a flagman. To live in a flagman's cottage outside the town would be good for his health.

The Governor, completely taken in by her manner, agreed. Frolenko and Lebedeva, two of her fellow-revolutionaries, then moved into the cottage as man and wife. The mine was prepared, but when the imperial train passed, nothing happened, for the dynamite had been faultily laid.

The attempted assassinations on the Losovaja-Sevastopol and the Moscow-Kursk lines were equally unsuccessful. For on the second route, the Tsar travelled in the first and not the second train, as Sofja Lvovna Perovskaja, who led this terrorist action, had been led to believe he would. This was a bitter disappointment, especially as innocent people were killed when the second train was derailed. Perovskaja, whose young face retained an expression of childlike innocence to the end, was later the first Russian woman revolutionary to be executed. She hated the Tsar more fiercely than many of her associates did. Perhaps this was so, because she knew his régime more intimately than did the others. Her family had always been very close to the government. She was a great-granddaughter of Sarumovski, the last Ukrainian Ataman, who had been Governor of the Crimea under Alexander I. Her father was Governor of St. Petersburg under Alexander II, the man whom she was determined to assassinate.

The assassinations planned late in 1879 and early in 1880 failed, as the attacks on the Tsar's train had

140 SEVEN WOMEN AGAINST THE WORLD

done. Stepan Chalturin, whom the Narodnaya Volya Party had entrusted with blowing up the Winter Palace, had not secured a sufficient amount of dynamite to carry out his plan effectively. A carpenter by trade, he was employed in the Tsar's household, and he had brought in the explosive in small quantities when he came to his work every morning.

Chalturin had been instructed to explode the Palace on the evening of February 5, 1880, when the Tsar was giving a large dinner-party for the Prince of Hesse, who had just arrived in Russia. Chalturin connected the fuse to the dynamite and left the Palace. When the Tsar and his guests entered the dining-room there was a terrible explosion, but only the room under the dining-room, where a guard regiment was stationed, was exploded. Again, a number of innocent people —the soldiers on duty—were killed, and the Tsar escaped, but this daring attempt, which was discussed with admiration all over Europe, made the Narodnaya Volya famous, and again won for its members much liberal support in Russia.

The Tsar now realized that the Narodnaya Volya was a very real danger. Immediately after the explosion in the Winter Palace a dictator, Count Moris-Melikov, was appointed. Mlodetzki made an unsuccessful attempt to assassinate him, and was executed. There is no question that the governing classes in Russia were profoundly shaken by these events. The Tsar, in fact, decided to issue a *ukase*, an imperial order, which was to introduce certain reforms in the administration of the country. Ironically enough he was later assassinated on the day on which he had officially proclaimed this *ukase*.

It was only natural that Vera Figner and her associates had no faith in these contemplated reforms, especially as after the attempted assassinations the police persecuted the subversive elements in the population more ruthlessly than ever. The number of

VERA FIGNER 141

arrests increased ; the Government was obviously panicky. Vera Figner's sister Eugenie and Alexander Michailov, a leader of the Narodnaya Volya, were among those who were arrested at this time. Eugenie was sent in exile to Siberia. The Tsarist Government had not yet decided to adopt the policy, a policy which subsequently made an unpleasant impression in Western Europe, of executing women as well as men who were members of revolutionary organizations.

After Chalturin's failure to blow up the Imperial family in the Winter Palace, the members of the Executive Committee of the Narodnaya Volya devoted themselves feverishly to new plans. During the next year a desperate and dramatic fight was waged for the life of the Tsar. The police strengthened their vigilance, their methods of intimidations ; while the revolutionaries, undaunted by their failure, spent days and nights deciding how to realize their intentions.

Perovskaja and Sablin, more practical than many of the other members, finally placed a careful plan before the Executive Committee of the Narodnaya Volya. The Tsar was expected to return to St. Petersburg in May, and it was decided to assassinate him when he drove from the centre of the city to the harbour. Vera Figner and her associates rented a little cheese shop in one of the streets through which he would pass. Perovskaja and Sablin were to pose as the shopkeeper and his wife. Business was to be carried on to conceal the real activities of the group.

A tunnel was to be dug from the shop to the centre of the road outside. Dynamite connected through the tunnel to the shop by a fuse was to be placed under the road. A revolutionary named Grigori Issajev, an engineer by profession, supervised the technical arrangements. Vera Figner's special assignment was to collect the money necessary for the building of the tunnel, for the rent of the shop, for the purchase of cheese and other goods which were offered for sale in the

142 SEVEN WOMEN AGAINST THE WORLD

ordinary way, and for the flight of the assassins after the Tsar had been killed.

As it was only a few weeks before the arrival of the Tsar, the revolutionaries faced a tremendous task. The soil under the shop was clayey, and progress was exasperatingly slow. The dug-up soil was carried into the shop and hidden in baskets, kegs, or parcels, as it would have roused the suspicion of the neighbours if it had been carried away. At the very last moment, however, a terrible accident made it impossible for the Narodnaya Volya to execute their plan: some dynamite exploded in Gregori Issajev's hand, tearing off three of his fingers. He was taken to hospital, and as the other inhabitants in the house had heard the detonation in the shop, any action had to be postponed indefinitely. They agreed to try again a year later.

On February 15, 1881, the Tsar's carriage drove past the cheese shop, but then, though the tunnel was completed, the explosive had not yet been laid. This time the revolutionaries refused to face defeat. Three definite plans were made to assassinate the Tsar. The next time the Tsar drove past the shop the fuse was to be lighted. In the event that the dynamite was faulty and the explosion did not take place, two of the members of the Executive Committee, armed with bombs, were to be stationed in the streets. Naturally they themselves would be killed if the dynamite under the road functioned properly, but personal danger meant nothing to these men and women. If these two plans failed, another of the group, armed with a dagger, was to attack the Tsar and stab him single-handed.

For some weeks it appeared as though none of these arrangements would be possible. Two very active members of the Narodnaya Volya, Trigoni and Sheljabov, the expert bomb-throwers of the group, were arrested. Besides, the police had discovered

VERA FIGNER 143

that some conspiracy against the Tsar was being plotted, and the authorities became suspicious of the district in which the cheese shop was situated. Each house in the district was searched, and in due course the police came to the shop. The floor next to one of the barrels containing fresh wet earth was very damp. The commissioner of police asked sharply what caused the dampness. One of the revolutionaries who was then acting as the shopkeeper, replied calmly that he had spilled some cream. The police were entirely satisfied with this answer, but naturally, with the entire street, the shop remained under surveillance.

A few days before the first of March, the day on which the assassination was to take place, Vera and her friends discovered to their horror that the fuse had not been laid. Besides, incredible as this seems, the four bombs had not yet been filled and made ready. In view of the fact that these ' Nihilists ' were ready to sacrifice their lives, this inefficiency is amazing.

Vera Figner and three of the men worked on the bombs all night from the last of February to the first of March. Perovskaja went to bed so that she would be rested for the tremendous strain she would undergo the next day.

At the last moment the Tsar chose a different route ; the explosive under the road, all their plans, in fact, had become meaningless. Perovskaja's mind worked quickly. Knowing that the imperial carriages would drive along the Katharina Canal, she ordered the men with the bombs to join her there. She told them where to stand and when to throw their bombs. At two o'clock in the afternoon Alexander II was assassinated.

Their success unnerved the members of the Narodnaya Volya, while their failures had left them relatively calm and determined. Most of the members of the Executive Committee were arrested ; one of

144 SEVEN WOMEN AGAINST THE WORLD

them committed suicide. They sent the letter with the Party's demands for reforms to the new Tsar, Alexander III, but the Party was too disorganized to take over the Government of the country.

'After the assassination of Alexander II,' Dr. Max Beer comments in this connection, 'the men in government circles had lost their heads to such an extent that if the Executive Committee of the Narodnaya Volya had been efficiently prepared, they might have been in a position to take over the government and to complete the political revolution, for liberal elements in Russia were sympathetic to the Party. The Party paid heavily for its sins of omission : the members themselves were tried and executed ; a brutal despot, Alexander III, followed Alexander II, and the new ruler was under the influence of that arch-reactionary Pobjedonostzev.'

It is difficult to agree unreservedly with Dr. Beer. All but eight of the original twenty-eight members of the Party were executed, exiled, or imprisoned after this assassination, and the remaining eight were suspect and could not move about freely to organize and instruct the new members. Where they had been wrong, of course, was in thinking that the population as a whole would support them. The masses were still too unenlightened and too intimidated to do so.

Perovskaja and the other ' Nihilists ' involved in the plot were executed on the third of April. It is a curious fact that the men and the woman hanged on this day represented all the classes of the Russian population : Sheljabov was a peasant ; Kibaltchitch the son of a priest ; Ryssakov came of ordinary middle-class stock ; Michailov was a workman ; and Perovskaja an aristocrat. They wore black robes, their hands were tied behind their backs, and they each wore a placard round their necks with the words : ' The murderer of a Tsar.' Perovskaja embraced all the men before the execution, with the exception of

VERA FIGNER

Ryssakov, who had given one of the Party's secret addresses to the police.

Immediately after the assassination, Perovskaja had stayed in Vera Figner's flat, so that, quite apart from her participation in the conspiracy, she had lain herself open to suspicion. 'Verotchka,' Perovskaja asked Vera Figner a few days before the police had finally tracked her down, 'may I sleep here in your flat?' Vera Figner remembers her own astonished answer: 'How can you ask? Doesn't this seem a matter of course to you?' Perovskaja said: 'I am merely asking, because if the police find me here you will be hanged too.' 'I put my arms round her,' Vera Figner writes, pointing to the revolver hanging at the foot of my bed, 'and I said: "I shall shoot whether they find you or not."'

Despite her fearless attitude, which made Vera Figner disregard her own danger, she was not found by the police for many months after the execution of her friends. Calling herself Helena Ivanovna Kolossova, she continued to work for her Party. She went first to Odessa, where she stayed for six months, and then to Moscow. Here she was finally arrested on February 10, 1883. She had been betrayed to the police by a former comrade, Wassili Merkulov, who had become a police informer.

She was taken to the Peter-Paul Prison in St. Petersburg to await her trial. One of the terroristic methods of the Tsarist Government was to keep political prisoners in custody for a long time before their trial, even when, obviously, a death sentence was expected. In many cases the prisoners' nerves were so shattered by this period of waiting and inactivity in solitary confinement that they broke down under repeated questioning and betrayed their friends.

Vera Figner was kept in the Peter-Paul Prison for twenty months. She believed that at her trial she would have her last opportunity of defending the social

146 SEVEN WOMEN AGAINST THE WORLD

revolution, and she was distressed to realize that, after several months of silence in her cell, her vocal chords began to weaken. In a similar situation many prisoners read aloud to themselves, but this possibility did not occur to her.

To keep her mind alert in her solitary confinement and to prevent herself from thinking, she sometimes spent the entire day studying a foreign language. She says that in two weeks she taught herself enough English to read Macaulay's *History of England*.

She was ready to die, and she resented a cruel destiny which forced her to go on living, alone and useless, until those in power were ready to execute her. ' I wanted to die,' she writes, ' I had to go on living so that I could appear before the court, where I could complete the last act in the career of an active revolutionary. As a member of the Executive Committee, I had my last words to say, my last duty to perform, just as all my predecessors had done. And as their comrade I had to share our common destiny to the end.'

She was tried on September 21, 1884, but instead of the death sentence she had hoped for and expected, she was sentenced to life imprisonment in Schluesselburg. This sentence was, of course, infinitely crueller than death, but the Tsarist Government did not have the courage of its convictions ; the régime did not want to appear inhumane by executing another woman.

Schluesselburg was the most terrible of Tsarist fortress prisons. It was built on an island in the river Neva, and the prisoners were cut off entirely from the mainland. There was no possible way of escape ; high walls surrounded the fortress, which could be reached only by boat. When Vera Figner went there, the prisoners were not allowed to write or receive letters from their friends or relatives ; once during the twenty years she spent in Schluesselburg she saw a newspaper, which had been brought into the

VERA FIGNER

fortress accidentally by an inspector. It was literally true of Schluesselburg that 'he who enters here leaves all hope behind.' 'Many prisoners are finally carried out of this prison dead,' as a Tsarist official once admitted, 'but few leave it on their own feet.'

Schluesselburg was situated in one of the most marshy and unhealthy parts in the Petersburg district ; the prison cells were damp, unclean, and verminous. A large percentage of the prisoners died of tuberculosis or scurvy. The food was very bad, and the prisoners were allowed only one short walk in the walled-in courtyard every day. The sanitary arrangements, if they can be called that, were quite indescribable.

The refinement of the cruelties practised in Schluesselburg surpassed the relentless harshness of other prisons in Tsarist Russia. For the first five years of Vera Figner's imprisonment, for instance, she was never given a sheet of paper or a pen, so that she did not even have the pitiful form of self-expression she might have derived from writing down her own thoughts. The staff of the prison was very large, and there were about twenty-five times as many warders and inspectors, all eager to exert their power, as there were prisoners.

Most of Vera Figner's fellow-prisoners died slow and agonizing deaths, and nothing was done to prevent the others from hearing their ghastly moans. Many of them lost their minds before they died, and the prison guards made sure that the other prisoners should witness this terrible process of mental disintegration. After Vera Figner had been buried alive at Schluesselburg for thirteen years and had lost all feeling of contact for the living in the outside world, she was suddenly instructed to write to her mother every six months. Probably the Government found it convenient at the time to proclaim that prisoners

148 SEVEN WOMEN AGAINST THE WORLD

at the fortress were in constant communication with their families.

It is tragic and impressive how these prisoners in Schluesselburg retained their human dignity. They were, of course, individuals of more than average social consciousness, or they would not have been willing to risk paying this terrible price for their convictions. Their unusual solidarity now found an outlet in their gallant loyalty to each other. It must have taken almost superhuman courage for them to strike, to give up their one short walk, when one prisoner had been locked up without food or drink in the darkened cell for some transgression against the prison rules of 1884 which still hung on the wall of each cell.

Vera Figner's position was in some ways more terrible than that of many of her comrades. For, apart from herself, there was only one other woman at Schluesselburg—Ludmilla Wolkenstein. These two women were carefully segregated from the men. They could talk only to each other. At Schluesselburg the daily half-hour walk round the gloomy courtyard with another prisoner was the only human companionship allowed them. The men could change their partners for the walk, but for years Vera and Ludmilla Wolkenstein were entirely alone.

If these prisoners could have known what was happening in the outside world their lives might not have been quite so tragic. They would have been able to follow the work of their successors in the social revolution. After the terrible reaction of the 'eighties, the movement took on new strength; and had the prisoners at Schluesselburg known this, they would at least have realized that their sacrifice had not been in vain. After Vera Figner had been at Schluesselburg for about eighteen years, the Goverment's growing fear of the social revolution was expressed in a slight improvement of prison conditions. Vera Figner

VERA FIGNER 149

began to hear about developments outside the fortress.

When she was at liberty the task of educating the masses of the Russian people seemed endless, a hope of the distant future. While she was at Schluesselburg, however, industry had developed in Russia, and the workers in the new factories, as well as many of the peasants, had joined the ranks of the revolutionaries. The intellectuals no longer bore the chief responsibility. In fact, as early as 1889, when the Second International met in Paris, and Plechanov and Lavrov represented the Russian labour movement, these two men concluded their report by declaring that ' the revolutionary intelligentsia of Russia was unable successfully to fight Tsarism, as they were still separated from the people. The Russian revolutionary movement will triumph only when it has become a mass movement.'

News was brought to Schuesselburg late in the 'nineties that a Social Democratic Party had been founded in Russia. This caused tremendous excitement among the prisoners. It is infinitely pathetic that these people, who had been completely isolated from reality, from the struggle to which they had once been utterly devoted, now began to argue about this new revolutionary Party. For they were obliged to discuss it purely theoretically. They had no background, no knowledge of the stages of the fight or the practical issues which had been at stake among their fellow-fighters for twenty years.

It is not surprising that when Vera Figner was amnestied and left Schluesselburg at 1904 she felt like a person who had been dead and who had returned to a life entirely unfamiliar to her. Her first contact with the living and normal world was, as one can so easily understand, a tremendous nervous shock to her. Unexpected noises, after the dull routine of the fortress, made her ill for days. She says in her *Memoirs*

150 SEVEN WOMEN AGAINST THE WORLD

that if any one dropped a silver teaspoon she had to exert all her self-control not to burst out crying, so terrible was the strain on her entire nervous system.

Her imprisonment in Schluesselburg was to be followed by exile in Siberia. When she was taken from the Peter-Paul Prison in St. Petersburg to the station, she peered curiously out of the window of the police van. She had the illusion that the men and women in the streets were wearing grey prisoners' suits or dresses. For twenty years she had seen nothing else. Nor could she see these ordinary people clearly ; their faces appeared to her as yellow smudges without distinct features.

At first it was little comfort to her gradually to understand what great strides the revolutionary movement had made in Russia. Old friends, whom she met in Siberia, and who had witnessed the terrible reaction of the 'eighties, told her that ' she had returned to life at the right time, at a time when the revolutionary movement was increasing rapidly.'

She found it difficult to believe that the first Revolution, which occurred a year after she left Schluesselburg, was already maturing in Russia. It was impossible for her to grasp this fact for many months. ' The basic factor of my life was Schluesselburg,' she writes sadly, ' the fortress robbed me of twenty years of my life. When it had separated me for so long, and without interruption, from the stream of events, it flung me out again—into another generation, new surroundings ; the logical economic and social development had completely changed conditions. I found it impossible to step over the evolution which had already occurred ; to step into these changed conditions, and to become assimilated into the new life. And that was my great misfortune.'

Vera Figner's temporary maladjustment might have been overcome more quickly had she not been exiled to Archangelsk, the most lonely and difficult of the

Siberian exile stations. Here the cold was terrible in the winter, and she was very much alone. Finally, in 1906, shortly after the first Russian Revolution, she was given permission by the Government to go abroad. She spent eight years in Switzerland and in Paris. She was too tired to take an active part in the Russian revolutionary movement, or to join Socialist exiles outside of Russia. Instead, she was engaged in winning support for a reform of Russian prison conditions. Like Louise Michel, in her old age, Vera Figner collected funds for prison reform. She published a pamphlet about Russian prisons, which was translated into many languages ; she wrote her *Memoirs*.

In 1914, when the War broke out, she returned to Russia, but she was arrested at the frontier and detained in Nishni Novgorod, where she had to report regularly to the police. Finally, in December 1916, she was permitted to go to St. Petersburg, where she witnessed the February Revolution. She was elected as chairman of an Amnesty Committee, and she helped the political prisoners who were released from the Tsarist prisons.

'The October Revolution,' she writes, ' made me very unhappy, as I had not expected the social upheavals which occurred. I had thought that a period in which our people would be gradually educated would precede the Revolution.'

Now Vera Figner is living in Moscow. She has become a legend of courage and conviction to the population of Russia. She herself is contented ; she is not bitter. ' Schluesselburg, with all its tribulations,' she writes, ' was not too great a price to pay for having belonged to an organization like the Executive Committee of the Narodnaya Volya, or for having participated in the fight waged by our Party against despotism.'

VI

EMMA GOLDMAN (1869-   )

No one who has heard or met Emma Goldman, the American Anarchist, can possibly doubt her sincerity, her absolute integrity of purpose or her humanity. In common with all anarchists, from Zeno, the Greek, to Proudhon, she is an extreme idealist, who fervently believes that human society can be governed without laws, that if state authority were abandoned the individual would develop personal initiative, and humanity would be free and happy.

'There are many,' as Emma Goldman herself admitted only last year in an article in *Harper's Magazine*, 'who deny the possibility of such regeneration on the ground that human nature cannot change.' She herself has never lost her faith that when anarchy has come humanity will eventually change for the better. She writes : ' I consider Anarchism the most beautiful and practical philosophy that has yet been thought of in its application to individual expression and the relation it establishes between the individual and society. Moreover, I am certain that Anarchism is too vital and too close to human nature ever to die.'

Though Emma Goldman's fundamental ideas have never altered, though she has never formulated her theories of the social upheaval in very definite terms, her outstanding personality has made her one of America's best known, most respected, and most feared women. A brilliant speaker and propagandist, she has consistently roused public interest and indignation against social injustice. Men and women of her type have functioned as an articulate conscience

154 SEVEN WOMEN AGAINST THE WORLD

for the United States. As a result, many policemen of all ranks have been made uneasy by her, for, though they may have stood for ' law and order,' few of them have had a record of personal integrity equal to hers. This fear of her was frequently reflected in the press. A leading article in the *New York Evening Sun* of September 30, 1909, for instance, makes the following statement about Emma Goldman :

' Emma Goldman is justly entitled to all the notoriety that is thrust upon her. She is perhaps not a clear-headed sociologist or even a very profound thinker ; her conceptions of the perfect State may be mistaken, and it is possible that the reforms she proposes are utterly absurd and ridiculous. Nevertheless, she has succeeded in presenting her opinions such as they are so forcibly as to throw the police all over the country into a veritable panic. . . . The popular belief is that she preaches bombs and murder, but she certainly does nothing of the kind. Bombs are very definite things, and one of the peculiarities of her doctrine is its vagueness. The wonder is that with a doctrine so vague she has managed to strike terror into the stout hearts of the police.'

One of the reasons, as this article shows, which has always made the authorities uncomfortable when they have dealt with her is Emma Goldman's inconspicuous appearance, which does not fit in with the popular conception of a wild-haired anarchist. At her trial during the War, the judge's remarks to the jury reflect his annoyance at her well-groomed presence. ' You think this woman before you is the real Emma Goldman,' she remembers him saying, ' this well-bred lady, courteous, and with a pleasant smile on her face ? No. The real Emma Goldman can be seen only on the platform. There she is in her true element, sweeping all caution to the winds. There she inflames the young and drives them to violent deeds. If you could see Emma Goldman at

EMMA GOLDMAN 155

her meetings, you would realize that she is a menace to our well-ordered institutions.'

Though Emma Goldman spent her childhood and early girlhood in Russia—she was twelve years old when Tsar Alexander was assassinated—she, like Vera Figner, did not begin to rebel against society until she was about twenty. Alexander Berkman, her fellow-anarchist, often jestingly ' gave his age minus the fourteen years ' he had spent in prison, and Emma Goldman would reply that ' the first twenty years of her life should not be held against her, for she had merely existed then.'

While Vera Figner's childhood had been so protected that she had no incentive to think about the injustices of the world, Emma Goldman's experience was exactly the opposite. Her childhood was harsh and unhappy ; economic uncertainty, hard work, and hatred of a cruel father prevented her young mind from dwelling on the world outside her immediate surroundings. It was not until she was many years older that she began to be sorry for her father and to ' regard him as one of the mass of the exploited and enslaved for whom she was living and working.'

Her family came from Popelan, in Courland. Her father was the manager of a relative's drapery shop. Abraham Goldman was ambitious for his many children ; he believed in discipline and a great deal of corporal punishment. When Emma was eight years old she was sent to Königsberg in East Prussia to live with her grandmother. Here she was to attend a good school and be well educated. Her grandmother, who owned a hairdressing shop, lived with Emma's uncle. After her grandmother left Königsberg, this uncle took the child out of school and she became the family drudge. For a girl so eager to learn and with so quick and receptive a mind, this must have meant a profound disappointment, quite apart from the fact that she was forced to work so hard that she became ill.

156 SEVEN WOMEN AGAINST THE WORLD

Finally, her parents heard about this state of affairs—Emma's uncle was spending the money sent for her education on himself—and they took her away from Königsberg. But this did not mean that life was less difficult. Her father had lost his job, and during the winter of 1882, when Emma was thirteen, she began to work in a factory in St. Petersburg.

At that time many Jews were leaving Russia, escaping from pogroms, and emigrating to the United States. Late in 1885 Emma and her sister Helena, to whom she was always deeply attached, went to Hamburg, and sailed from there as steerage passengers for America. One of their elder sisters had already settled in the United States, and the two girls joined her and her husband in Rochester, in the State of New York.

Emma found employment as a sewing girl in a factory in Rochester, where conditions were extremely bad. She worked ten and a half hours a day for a wage of $2.50—that is, ten shillings a week—and the working week consisted of sixty-three hours.

It must have been a shock to Emma Goldman to realize that America was by no means the Utopia it had seemed at a distance, when she had thought about it in Russia. The illusions harboured about the United States by so many immigrants from Eastern Europe is easy to understand. In Russia the growing struggle of the working class was directed against privileges of birth and class. The so-called lower classes were oppressed because they had been born into a certain order ; their fight was largely political. In the United States, on the other hand, where these class distinctions did not exist, the development of industry had caused the rich to exploit the poor, regardless of the class into which either of them had been born. The conflict was between capital and labour, and Emma Goldman was soon to realize that oppression could be quite as ruthless, or more so, in a politically

EMMA GOLDMAN 157

democratic country as in a country dominated by the despotism of a Tsar.

'On coming to America,' Emma Goldman writes, 'I had the same hopes as have most European immigrants and the same disillusionment, though the latter affected me more keenly and more deeply. The immigrant without money and without connexions is not permitted to cherish the comfortable illusion that America is a benevolent uncle who assumes a tender and impartial guardianship of nephews and nieces. I soon learned that in a republic there are a myriad ways by which the strong, the cunning, the rich can seize power and hold it. I saw the many work for small wages which kept them always on the borderline of want for the few who made huge profits. I saw the courts, the halls of legislation, the press, and the schools—in fact, every avenue of education and protection—effectively used as an instrument for the safeguarding of a minority, while the masses were denied every right.'

Apart from her political disillusionment, Emma Goldman suffered a personal disappointment while she was in Rochester. In 1888 she married Jacob Kershner, who had come to the United States from Odessa a few years before. She had hoped to have much in common with him, but the marriage was a failure and she soon left him. Her parents, who had emigrated to America in 1886, were horrified when she did so, but her emancipation from them was now complete.

Already she was beginning to live chiefly for her Cause, that of Anarchism, the abolishment of all laws. It is possible that had Emma Goldman seen more clearly, had she been attracted by a more constructive form of revolutionary thought, had she and her friends believed in a socialistic form of government which would have replaced the old order in America, they might have had a considerable influence, and the

158 SEVEN WOMEN AGAINST THE WORLD

labour movement in that country might have taken a
different course. For her courage, her unselfish
devotion to her principles, even when, as a young
woman, she was still living in Rochester, were
magnificent.

A little later Emma Goldman and the group of
fervent young anarchists round her determined to
' dedicate themselves to the Cause in some supreme
deed, to die together if necessary, or to live and work
for the ideal for which one of them might have to
give his life.' Their feeling of personal duty towards
Anarchism, so this passage seems to indicate, was
more important than Anarchism itself. In our
generation, when we hear so much of State planning,
it is understandable that, as a reaction, some individuals are attracted by anarchist doctrines. In the
'eighties and 'nineties of the last century, however,
especially in the United States, there was much constructive organization to be done in the growing
labour movement, and it is astonishing that a woman
as clever and as sincere as Emma Goldman could have
been so unpractical.

The outstanding conflict between capital and labour
at this period, an event which influenced Emma
Goldman's entire career, was the famous Haymarket
Case of 1886. The workers of the McCormick
Harvester Company of Chicago, who were protesting
against low wages and bad working conditions, met in
Haymarket Square in Chicago on the fourth of May.
The demonstration was peaceful ; the Mayor of the
city came himself to see that the meeting passed off
without disturbances. After he left, a police officer,
a Captain Ward, dispersed the crowd by force, thus
creating a riot. During the skirmish a bomb was
exploded, but it was never satisfactorily proven who
committed this act of violence. Eight men, five of
whom were anarchists, were arrested. The State of
Illinois was never able to establish their guilt, but

EMMA GOLDMAN 159

these eight men were executed on the eleventh of November 1887, and for years afterwards anarchists all over the world made this day one of commemoration.

'This judicial crime,' Emma Goldman writes, 'left an indelible mark on my mind and heart, and sent me forth to acquaint myself with the ideal for which these men had died so heroically. I dedicated myself to their cause.'

She determined to become an active anarchist. With this aim constantly before her she went to New York, arriving there on her twentieth birthday, August 15, 1889. Her possessions when she reached New York consisted of five dollars, a small handbag, a sewing machine, an ability for hard work, and her devotion to the doctrine in which she believed.

When she reached New York, friends took her at once to Sachs' Café in Suffolk Street, the meeting-place of socialists, radicals, and other progressive men and women. Here she met Johann Most, a former member of the German Reichstag, who was then editing the anarchist newspaper *Freiheit*, and the first evening she spent at Sachs' Café she saw Alexander Berkman, then a fiery youth of eighteen, with whom she has been closely associated throughout her life.

In New York Emma found employment in a corset factory, and later in a blouse factory, but already she was devoting herself largely to her political activities. Johann Most appreciated the tremenous possibilities of this brilliant young woman at once, and encouraged her work. When she had been in New York for six months she began her career as a public speaker ; she addressed meetings in Rochester and Buffalo. She was still very nervous whenever she spoke to large audiences, and she could hardly have realized that, one day, she would become one of the finest and most compelling speakers in America.

160 SEVEN WOMEN AGAINST THE WORLD

In 1890, George Kennan, an American journalist, went to Russia and roused the indignation of liberals in the United States with his accounts of the terrible conditions prevailing among the political exiles in Siberia. A society, known as the American Friends of Russian Freedom, was organized. Emma Goldman was deeply interested. She planned to return to Russia and to take part in the illegal political movement of her native country. She and Berkman went to New Haven, where they learned printing, so that they would be able to publish illegal literature in Russia. They then moved to Worcester, in the state of New York, where they opened what Americans call an 'ice-cream parlour.' They were thus earning money to finance their journey to Russia.

Serious labour troubles in the Carnegie Steel Company, however, caused them to change their plans very suddenly. High tariffs on imported steel had resulted in a boom in the industry ; and in view of the rising profits, the workers, quite naturally, demanded higher wages. The new wage scale presented by the Amalgamated Association of Iron and Steel Workers was, however, rejected by the Carnegie Steel Company, and a strike was called in May 1892. Pinkerton's private army, one of the most deplorable institutions of American industrial life, was engaged by the Steel Company to suppress the strike, which occurred in Homestead, near Pittsburg, at the Company's largest mill. Pinkerton's men opened fire on the workers, and a battle—if such a term can be used when only one side was armed—began. Carnegie himself was rarely seen at Homestead, and the workers' hatred centred round Henry Clay Frick, the chairman of the Company.

When Emma Goldman and Berkman heard what was happening in Homestead they left Worcester at once. In a few hours they had settled their affairs, paid their bills and left, taking only the day's earnings with them.

EMMA GOLDMAN 161

Berkmen harboured the pathetic belief that the steel workers would be helped if he killed Frick. These anarchists could not understand that the removal of a few individuals would not bring about a change in the industrial system. 'Frick,' Emma Goldman wrote, was 'the symbol of wealth and power, of the injustice and wrong of the capitalistic class.'

Emma Goldman and Berkman went to New York to prepare the attack on Frick. None of these ardent and theoretical young anarchists had ever manufactured bombs, but they studied Most's *Science of Revolution*, and with the help of this book they set to work with explosives.

Emma Goldman wanted desperately to go to Homestead with Berkman, but she had no money for the journey. Her fanatic and loyal desire to share the dangers with him, and to risk everything for her cause, prompted her to walk the streets at night, resolved to make enough money during the one night for the journey. 'On Saturday evening, July 16, 1892,' she writes, 'I walked up and down 14th Street, one of the long procession of girls I had so often seen plying their trade.' In the end, however, she went home, unable to carry out her intentions. For like many women who live and preach an unconventional personal life, she was particularly discriminating.

Berkman went to Homestead and found his way into Frick's office. In the end he used a pistol instead of his bombs. When the shot failed to kill Frick, Berkman attacked him with a knife, fighting desperately. Frick was badly wounded, but in the end he recovered. For Berkman the most tragic phase of this affair was the fact that some of the workers, whom he thought he was helping, rushed in and rescued their employer from the fatal blow.

'Young man by the name of Berkman,' the New York papers announced in glaring headlines, 'shoots Frick. Assassin overpowered by working men.'

162 SEVEN WOMEN AGAINST THE WORLD

Berkmen was sentenced to twenty-two years penal servitude in the Pennsylvania Penitentiary, where conditions were particularly inhuman. For years Emma Goldman and Berkman's other friends lodged appeals, hoping to attain a pardon for him. Her tireless and unsuccessful efforts to free him became one of the important activities of her life. Until her ruse was discovered she was allowed to visit Berkman in prison, for she posed as his sister.

After Berkman's arrest, Emma Goldman's flat had been raided by the police, but she had removed the dynamite she had been storing and of all other evidence of her association with Berkman. The police could not prove anything against her, but from that time onward they were constantly suspicious of her. She began to be known as ' Red Emma.' Obviously the authorities were looking forward to the time when they could send her to prison, at least for a long period.

At this time the Federal and the State Governments had particular cause to fear radicals of Emma Goldman's type. The industrial crisis, the ' Panic of 1893,' had created tremendous unrest among labour ; riots occurred in many cities ; the famous Pullman Car Company's strike in Chicago in 1894 was merely one of the many active revolts organized by the workers.

Emma Goldman, now recognized as a brilliant speaker, addressed labour meetings everywhere, encouraging the working men and women to take action. She was finally arrested in Philadelphia, charged with inciting a crowd to riot on three counts. She was sent for a year to the women's prison on Blackwell Island.

While she was in prison Emma Goldman became interested in nursing, and she assisted the doctors in the prison hospital. Shortly after she was released, in August 1895, Edward Brady and some of her other friends arranged for her to go to Vienna to take up

EMMA GOLDMAN 163

nursing seriously. She had found that it was impossible to carry on her strenuous political work and her public speaking without a regular profession, which could provide her with at least enough money to have sufficient food and rest. In Vienna, where she entered the *Allgemeines Krankenhaus*, she was known as Mrs. E. G. Brady.

She went to London on her way to Vienna, and her meeting with English anarchists and Russians living as exiles in England revived her after the weary months in prison. She frequently saw Louise Michel in London, and of her she writes : ' She was angular, gaunt, aged before her years, but there was a spirit and youth in her eyes, and a smile so tender that it immediately won my heart.'

When Emma Goldman returned to New York, a qualified midwife and nurse, and from all accounts a particularly efficient one, she was economically freer, despite her hard work, to devote her energy to her political plans. In the late 'nineties, apart from her continuous efforts in connexion with the Alexander Berkman Defence Association, she made it her business to rouse public feeling in the United States against social injustices which were occurring in various parts of the world. In 1896, for instance, when three hundred men and women were arrested and tortured in the Spanish Prison of Montjuich after a bomb explosion in Barcelona, she spoke in many American cities about this terror.

Not only did she organize meetings to protest against definite acts of injustice; she toured the country lecturing about general subjects, all of which she interpreted from the anarchist point of view. ' New Women,' one of her lectures was called ; ' Freedom,' ' Charity,' ' Absurdity of Non-Resistance to Evil,' ' Patriotism,' ' The Basis of Morality ' were others.

During the late 'nineties great economic changes were occurring in the United States. While the

164 SEVEN WOMEN AGAINST THE WORLD

depression lasted, many large and solvent firms had bought up their smaller rivals; and powerful monopolies, such as the Standard Oil Company, were beginning to exert a decisive influence on American industry as a whole, and on labour conditions in particular. The United States were fast becoming the outstanding example of the capitalist State against which Emma Goldman had been rebelling all her life.

There was less chance than there ever had been to turn this vast governmental machine into a country without a government. Such a hope, to which the anarchists clung as fiercely as ever, had become more fantastic still. They continued valiantly, however, to hope that they would sweep away the government, any government, by removing its leaders, and in the summer of 1909 President William McKinley was shot while he was visiting the Pan-American Exposition in Buffalo. The assassin, a young anarchist named Leon Czolgosz, was not known to Emma Goldman, but she was now so generally feared as the instigator of all anarchist plots that she was drawn into his trial.

She had been lecturing in Saint Louis, and was walking calmly down the road, when she was suddenly confronted with the following headline of a St. Louis newspaper, 'Assassin of President McKinley an anarchist. Confesses to having been incited by Emma Goldman, woman anarchist, who is wanted by the police.' Emma herself, who knew nothing whatsoever about Czolgosz's attack until she saw the newspapers, was staggered. She acted quickly and went to Chicago. Some friends, who were not known to have any connections with the anarchists, took her into their home.

While she was in hiding and being looked for by the police—and this could happen only in the United States—the *Chicago Tribune* announced that they would pay her five thousand dollars for an interview, and not hand her over to the authorities, if she would

EMMA GOLDMAN 165

communicate with the paper where a reporter could find her.

She needed this money badly for her coming trial, so her hosts went to the *Chicago Tribune* offices to bring back the reporter. She planned to give herself up to the police as soon as she had received the payment for her interview, for, had the police become suspicious of her friends, they would have been arrested for taking her to their home.

The police, however, already suspected where she was. While her friends were away to fetch the reporter, twelve policemen appeared at the house. Emma posed as a Swedish maid who knew little English, and at first the police were taken in. Then, much to her annoyance, they found a fountain-pen on the table with her name engraved on it, and she was arrested and taken into custody at once.

The weeks she spent in prison before her lawyers finally proved without a doubt that she had nothing to do with the assassination of President McKinley were one of the most depressing periods of her life. Her desperate attempts to save Leon Czolgosz from execution failed. For the first time in her life she was assailed by doubts about the theories of Anarchism. ' Our movement,' she wrote at this time, ' had lost its appeal to me ; many of its adherents filled me with loathing. They had been flaunting Anarchism like a red cloth before a bull, but they ran to cover at its first charge. I could no longer work with them.'

Her depression increased when she was released from prison. Her life was extremely hard and bitter. Though she called herself Miss E. G. Smith, she did not succeed in hiding her identity for long, and landladies refused to let her stay in their lodging-houses. Finally, she and her brother Yegor, to whom she was always devoted, took a flat together.

Professionally, too, her association in the mind of the public with the President's assassination did her

166 SEVEN WOMEN AGAINST THE WORLD

great harm. With very few exceptions, physicians, who had formerly recommended her to their patients as a nurse, no longer sent cases to her. She was again forced to accept home work from clothing manufacturers, and to earn her living as a sewing girl.

Her puzzling doubts concerning anarchy, the troubling questions she was asking herself about the form this doctrine should take, were not relieved by a letter Alexander Berkman sent to her from the Penitentiary.

'The scheme of political subjection is subtle in America,' he wrote. 'Though McKinley was the chief representative of our modern slavery, he could not be considered in the light of a direct and immediate enemy of the people. In an absolutism the autocrat is visible and tangible. The real despotism of republican institutions is far deeper, more insiduous, because it rests on the popular delusion of self-government and independence. That is the source of democratic tyranny, and as such it cannot be reached with a bullet. In modern capitalism economic exploitation rather than political oppression is the real enemy of the people. Politics are but its handmaid. Hence the battle is to be waged in the economic rather than the political field. It is therefore that I regard my own act as far more significant and educational than Leon's. It was directed against a tangible, real oppressor, visualized as such by the people.'

These theoretical considerations of Berkman, Goldman, and other American anarchists did not affect the Government's policy towards them, and President Roosevelt's anti-anarchist legislation dealt harshly with them. Yet even this ' mad pack howling for their lives ' did not at first rouse Emma Goldman. ' She remained benumbed and inert, unable to do anything except torment herself with everlasting whys and wherefores.'

EMMA GOLDMAN 167

Despite the Government's growing antagonism towards the radical elements in the country, and the country's fear, sometimes bordering on hysteria, of subversive opinion, the next few years were among the most peaceful of Emma Goldman's life. She solved her professional problems by opening a massage shop, and she ' finally emerged from her tortuous introspection as from a long illness, not yet in possession of her former vigour, but with a determination to try once more to steel her will to meet the exigences of life, whatsoever they might be.'

One of the reasons why she was not worried by the police as much as usual during the early years of the century was her interest in the growing revolutionary movement in Russia. Naturally the United States Government was not concerned if she spread subversive teachings about other countries. She went on a lecture tour, speaking about Russia, and was in close connexion with the Society of the Friends of Russian Freedom. She co-operated with a Russian who came from Russia on behalf of the Social Revolutionary Party, though, of course, as he believed in a socialist State, she, who believed in a stateless form of society, must have disagreed with him fundamentally. She was excited and hopeful early in 1905, the year of the first Russian Revolution, and she was a great admirer of Babuschka, the ' grandmother of the Russian Revolution,' who was then in New York.

'At the Russians' New Year's ball,' Emma Goldman wrote many years later, ' we greeted the advent of 1905 standing in a circle, Babuschka dancing the *kazatchok* with one of the boys. It was a feast for the eyes to see this woman of sixty-two, her spirit young, cheeks ruddy, and eyes flashing, whirling about in the popular Russian dance.'

At this time Emma Goldman began to publish the periodical *Mother Earth*, and she became in-

168 SEVEN WOMEN AGAINST THE WORLD

terested in the drama. In 1906, when Alexander Berkman, whose sentence had been commuted to thirteen years' penal servitude, was released, she devoted herself to him, helping him to adjust himself again to a free life. When no publisher was courageous enough to publish his prison memoirs, she arranged to do so herself.

In 1909 she planned to go to Australia, but on some flimsy technical grounds the United States Government refused to give her a passport. She was thus forced to give up the Australian journey. She took up the McNamara case in San Francisco, though she fundamentally disagreed with McNamara, who, so she believed, was a trade-unionist, ' who saw in their (the workers') struggle no more than a feud between their organization and the steel interests.'

Her untiring efforts on behalf of McNamara reflect her broadmindedness. Emma Goldman has always courageously defended those whom she considered oppressed or unjustly treated—and in her judgment of such cases of social injustices she was usually right—even though the unfortunate people concerned did not share her views and were not anarchists. She supported the meetings of the unemployed workers during the panic of 1907. She worked for the hop-pickers who had gone to the hopfields of Wheatfield, in California, in answer to advertisements. They had organized a strike when they found that they had been tricked into intolerable working conditions, and they were then shot at by a private army hurried to the spot by their employer. She roused public interest in the fate of the striking coal-miners in the famous strikes at Ludlow, in Colorado.

Her real persecution began with the outbreak of the War. Before the United States took part in the hostilities, her anti-war meetings were not broken up by the police, but at that time her work for the birth-

EMMA GOLDMAN 169

control movement was causing the Government to watch her closely. She was finally arrested and sent to prison for a short time, as she preferred incarceration to paying a fine. In this choice she showed her unerring instinct for giving publicity to her causes. An enormous meeting was held in the Carnegie Hall by other supporters of birth control to protest against her arrest, and this meeting roused public interest in the movement throughout the country.

When the United States joined the Allies, Emma Goldman concentrated her energies on anti-war propaganda. She was an active member of the Non-Conscription League. Sections of the American press became quite hysterical whenever her lack of patriotism was mentioned. She was accused of receiving money from the German Emperor for her anti-war propaganda. Typically American headlines appeared : ' Kaiser gives Goldman money ' was one of them.

Emma Goldman recalls one large meeting, held on May 18, 1917, at the Harlem River Casino, which was attended by ten thousand people. Many soldiers, in very new uniforms, had come to break up this pacifist gathering. They interrupted the speakers, and finally one young soldier rose and demanded to speak. The pacifist audience objected strenuously, and a motion was carried to remove this young soldier from the hall. Emma Goldman as usual kept her head.

' Raising my voice,' she writes, ' I appealed to the assembly to permit the man to speak. " We who have come here to protest against coercion and to demand the right to think and act in accordance with our consciences," I urged, " should recognize the right of an opponent to speak, and we should listen quietly and grant him the respect we demand for ourselves. The young man no doubt believes in the justice of his cause as we do in ours, and he has pledged his

170 SEVEN WOMEN AGAINST THE WORLD

life for it. I suggest, therefore, that we all rise in appreciation of his evident sincerity and that we hear him out in silence." The audience rose to a man.'

' The soldier,' Emma Goldman continues in her *Living My Life*, ' had probably never before faced such a large assembly. He looked frightened, and he began in a quavering voice that barely carried to the platform, although he was sitting near it. He stammered something about " German money " and " traitors," got confused, and came to a sudden stop. Then, turning to his comrades, he cried: " Oh, hell, let's get out of here." Out the whole gang slunk, waving their little flags and followed by laughter and applause.'

Naturally Emma Goldman's presence of mind, and the fact that she had made the young soldiers appear ridiculous did not make her any more popular, but this incident was not serious. The Government was far more incensed by her unceasing defence of Tom Mooney, who had been arrested and condemned to death after the bomb explosion during a Preparedness Parade in San Francisco in July 1916. Emma Goldman happened to be in San Francisco at the time with Alexander Berkman, who was publishing the *Blast*, a new anarchist paper, in California.

The police had been antagonistic towards Thomas Mooney, a member of the Moulders' Union, for a long time, and it was obvious that they were glad to arrest him on the charge of throwing the bomb. Emma Goldman and Alexander Berkman's energetic and uncompromising support of Mooney—whose death sentence was finally commuted to one of life imprisonment—made the authorities still more antagonistic towards their anti-war campaign.

They were arrested in the *Mother Earth* offices in June 1917 and brought to trial on the seventh of the month, Emma Goldman's forty-eighth birthday.

This trial was a typical example of the war fever which prevailed in the United States. It is probably inevitable that those countries which are farthest away from the actual scene of the conflict, are always most frightened of its dangers.

The prosecution quite unfairly brought up what Emma Goldman had said before May 18, 1917, when conscription became a law. The question as to where her money came from was discussed at length. When an American of considerable wealth and radical views, James Halbeck, testified that he had supplied the funds for Emma Goldman's campaign the court was obviously annoyed.

The trial was a sensation for the press. A recruiting station was opened in the street below the courthouse, so that, appalled by the example of those being tried within, young men would volunteer for war service. On one day—and the trial lasted for several—the Russian Soviet Mission, playing the Marseillaise, marched past the building. Reporters crowded the press gallery ; the proceedings were a front-page story.

Berkman and Emma Goldman were sentenced to two years penal servitude and to a fine of $10,000 each. He was sent to the Penitentiary at Atlanta, Georgia, and she to the one at Jefferson, Missouri. When she had been there two weeks, Justice Louis D. Brandeis of the United States Supreme Court, one of the most courageous Americans who has ever lived, signed an appeal for the reconsideration of her case. This meant that she could be free on bail until the appeal came before the Supreme Court. As was to be expected, this appeal was refused, and Emma Goldman spent two years in the Penitentiary.

Some weeks before their conviction, knowing that they would eventually be imprisoned for their views, Emma Goldman and Alexander Berkman had published a statement in the *Mother Earth Bulletin* which re-

172 SEVEN WOMEN AGAINST THE WORLD

flected the indomitable courage with which they went to prison :

'Be of good cheer, friends and comrades,' they wrote, 'We are going to prison with light hearts. To us it is more satisfactory to stay behind bars than to remain muzzled in freedom. Our spirit will not be daunted, nor our will broken. We will return to our work in due time.

'This is our farewell to you. The light of Liberty burns low just now. But do not despair, friends. Keep the spark alive. The night cannot last for ever. Soon there will come a rift in the darkness, and the New Day break even in this country. May each of us feel that we have contributed our mite toward the great Awakening.

'EMMA GOLDMAN
'ALEXANDER BERKMAN.'

For an active woman of Emma Goldman's age these two years in the Penitentiary must have presented unspeakable hardships. She had not performed strenuous manual work for some years, and the cruel 'tasks' demanded daily of the women in the sewing shops in the Jefferson Penitentiary were a great physical strain even for the younger women. Emma Goldman devoted herself to the other prisoners ; she wrote letters to her friends telling them of the conditions at Jefferson.

While she was in prison she also suffered a great personal grief. Her sister Helena's son, David Hochstein, a talented violinist, had volunteered for war service and was killed in France in 1918.

At the Penitentiary, and before her arrest, Emma Goldman had followed developments in Russia. She welcomed the Russian Revolution despite the fact that, as an anarchist, she did not agree with the Bolsheviki. From her point of view there was a

EMMA GOLDMAN

tremendous danger in the dictatorship of the proletariat, but she defended the new government in Russia against attacks from many of her anarchist friends. Some of them ‘ thought that the Bolsheviki, representing a government, should be treated by anarchists like other governments.’ Emma Goldman, however, ‘ insisted that Soviet Russia, the object of attack by the combined reactionists of the world, was not at all to be considered as an ordinary government.’ She did not ‘ object to criticism of the Bolsheviki, but she did not approve active opposition to them, anyway not until they should be in a less dangerous situation.’ In all her public and private utterances before her arrest Emma Goldman was a staunch supporter of the new Russia.

‘ Though they were Marxists and therefore governmentalists,’ she declared, ‘ I sided with them because they had repudiated war and had the wisdom to stress the fact that political freedom without corresponding economic equality is an empty boast.’ This fact she had learned from experience after living for twenty-eight years in the United States.

Neither she nor Berkman, however, seriously contemplated returning to Russia after the Revolution. They were both too deeply attached to the United States. Patriots in the best sense of the word, they still longed to realize the political and economic ideas in which they so firmly believed in their adopted country. Besides, at the time, they were both determined to help save Thomas Mooney’s life, and they felt that to leave the United States would have meant deserting him.

Emma Goldman was released from prison in September 1919. She and Berkman had each been allowed four months off their sentence for good behaviour, but both served another month instead of the huge fine which had been a part of their sentence and which of course they could not pay. The United

174 SEVEN WOMEN AGAINST THE WORLD

States Immigration Bureau took over Emma Goldman's case after she left the Penitentiary, and she was allowed to move about freely after a bail of fifteen thousand dollars had been paid for her by friends.

The Immigration Bureau's interest made it quite clear that Berkman and Goldman might be deported from the United States at any moment, especially as he had never been given an American passport.

At Emma Goldman's hearing before officials from the Immigration Bureau she refused to answer any questions, as she agreed with Alexander Berkman that her social ' views and political opinions were her personal concern.' She believed that she owed no one an explanation of them, ' that responsibility begins only with the effect of thought expressed in action.'

At the end of this one-sided interrogation she gave the officials a written statement expressing her point of view, and this statement is illuminating, for it shows that Emma Goldman's ' anarchy.' has, at times, been closer to the principles of real democracy than she herself might admit.

' If the present proceedings,' she had written, ' are for the purpose of proving some alleged offence committed by me, some evil or anti-social act, then I protest against the secrecy and third-degree methods of this so-called " trial." But if I am not charged with any specific offence or act, if—as I have reason to believe—this is purely an inquiry into my social and political opinions, then I protest still more vigorously against these proceedings, as utterly tyrannical and diametrically opposed to the fundamental guarantees of a true democracy. Every human being is entitled to hold any opinion that appeals to her or him without making herself or himself liable to persecution . . .

' The free expression of the hopes and aspirations of a people is the greatest and only safety in a sane society. In truth, it is such free expression and discussion alone that can point the most beneficial path for human progress and development. But the object of deportations and of the Anti-Anarchist Law, as of all similar repressive measures, is the very opposite. It is to stifle the voice of the people, to muzzle every aspiration of labour. That is the real and terrible menace of the star-chamber proceedings of the tendency of exiling those who do not fit into the scheme of things our industrial lords are so eager to perpetuate.

'With all the power and intensity of my being I protest against the conspiracy of imperialist capitalism against the life and the liberty of the American people.'

Her gallant defence of her position was of no help, and Emma Goldman was ordered to report at Ellis Island for deportation on the fifth of December. She and Berkman spent the weeks before this date lecturing in many cities of the United States about Soviet Russia. By a curious irony of fate, the news of Henry Clay Frick's death, the man whom Berkman had attempted to kill so many years before, reached them in Chicago on the second of December while they were attending a farewell dinner before leaving for Ellis Island. Frick died peacefully in his bed, while Berkman was on the eve of his deportation from the United States, but this fact did not depress either Berkman or Emma Goldman. They had never thought in terms of failure.

Emma Goldman had one more opportunity of telling the people of the United States about another evil in their social life : Ellis Island, where immigrants were often held for weeks and where conditions must have been, or still are, a disgrace. This was to be her last public effort to awaken the conscience of the men and women who had been her countrymen.

They were her countrymen no longer. She and Berkman, with many others, were deported from

176 SEVEN WOMEN AGAINST THE WORLD

Ellis Island on December 20, 1919. In close and poorly ventilated quarters, the deportees, supervised by rude immigration officers, sailed for Europe in the *Buford*. She was an old unsteady vessel, and had been used for the transportation of soldiers during the Spanish American War. Friction was soon felt between the deportees and the government officials, and Berkman, as an informal spokesman of the men and women being deported, finally succeeded in bringing about a slight improvement of their conditions on the ship.

The journey lasted twenty-eight days, and the unseaworthy old ship was so badly damaged by the time she reached Kiel Canal that she stopped for a day and a night for repairs. The deportees were locked up in their quarters, but when a German barge came alongside the vessel Emma Goldman threw out a letter addressed to the periodical published by the Independent Socialist Party of Germany, in which she urged the members to ' make their revolution as fundamental as the Russian.' Nothing, not even a long and miserable journey on this old vessel, could dampen her enthusiasm for her cause, nothing could lessen her instinct to give it publicity whenever there was the slightest chance to do so.

In January, the *Buford* finally docked at Hango, a Finnish port. Each deportee was given three days' rations and they were then turned over to the Finnish authorities. In a guarded train they were taken to Teryoki, on the Russian frontier, where they were met by representatives of the Soviet Government.

Emma Goldman was in a state of intense excitement when she crossed the border and entered Soviet Russia. Her capacity for enthusiasm, for faith, and her vitality, are the most remarkable characteristics of this remarkable woman. For years her life had consisted of lecture tours, which meant catching trains, travelling at night, meeting new people ; of

EMMA GOLDMAN 177

persecution ; of family anxieties culminating in the loss of her nephew. She had spent two terrible years in prison ; miserable days and nights on Ellis Island. She had been on a rough sea on the *Buford* for weeks, but when she reached Russia at last, she was buoyant. She is one of those rare individuals who is never too old to begin a new life.

At first she was lyrical about Russia. ' Soviet Russia,' she writes, ' sacred ground, magic people. You have come to symbolize humanity's hope, you alone are destined to redeem mankind. I have come to serve you, beloved *matushka*. Take me to your bosom, let me pour myself into you, mingle my blood with yours, find my place in your heroic struggle, and give to the uttermost to your needs.'

Emma Goldman and Berkman were in Russia until November 1921. She had been in America for so long that at first she had difficulty in speaking and understanding Russian, but soon this language of her childhood came back to her. She was then able to talk to the workers, to every one she met, without an interpreter. She had an opportunity of discussing the new Russia with many of the men and women who were responsible for the country's development : Lenin, Litvinoff, Gorki, and she had secret meetings with those who were unpopular with the new régime : Spiridonova and other Social Revolutionaries, Peter Kropotkin, and other anarchists.

Emma Goldman arrived in Russia with more than an open mind. She was prepared to spend the rest of her life in this country, and to contribute towards the building up of the new State. She longed to do constructive work and she was not satisfied with the relatively trivial tasks assigned to her by the Bolsheviki. She helped to organize the reception of communist refugees from the United States, she and Berkman travelled all over Russia collecting material for the Museum of the Revolution. She suggested

178 SEVEN WOMEN AGAINST THE WORLD

to Lenin in a personal interview that she establish a Society of Russian Friends for American Freedom, just as, in the United States, she had co-operated with the Society of American Friends of Russian Freedom.

From the start, however, she met with considerable antagonism. The makers of the Russian Revolution were harsh realists, who firmly believed that there can be no revolution without violence and a terror. Emma Goldman had always believed in violence in theory, and in practice, too; she had, for instance, given Berkman her moral support when he tried to assassinate Frick. But she was an indomitable idealist who thought that once the revolution had been fought, the terror must cease; every one should be more or less free to express his individual opinions and to act accordingly. She did not recognize the fact, proven by every revolution in history, that such upheavals and the cruelty and violence they involve, cannot stop as soon as the leaders of the revolution are technically in power. She longed to be closer to the ' toiling masses,' thinking of them more as an articulate and definite entity than as a vast and illiterate population.

Her attitude towards Russia reflected Emma Goldman's absolute integrity and honesty. It would have been easy enough for her to overlook the phases of the Revolution which distressed her. Honour, position, and plenty of constructive work would have been hers if she had agreed with the Bolsheviki. Her courageous attack on them is all the more admirable, as Russia was the only country open to her. If she was deported, so she knew, she would be forced to drift about Europe a homeless refugee.

Her mental conflict haunted her for months. ' I was ready to admit frankly,' she wrote, ' that I had erred grievously when I had defended Lenin and his party as the true champions of the Revolution. But

I would not engage in active opposition to them so long as Russia was still being attacked by outside enemies. I was no longer deceived by their mask, but my real problem lay much deeper. It was the Revolution itself. Its manifestations were so completely at variance with what I had conceived and propagated as revolution that I did not know any more which was right. My old values had been shipwrecked, and I myself thrown overboard to sink or swim. All I could do was to try to keep my head above water and trust to time to bring me to safe shores.'

During the Kronstadt Rebellion, which ended on March 17, 1921, Emma Goldman decided that she must speak. In a manifesto to the Petrograd Soviet Labour and Defence Committee, of which Zinoviev was chairman, she, Berkman, and two Russian Anarchists declared that ' To remain silent now is impossible, even criminal.' They warned the Soviet Government that the policy of fighting the Kronstadt workers, instead of trying to conciliate them, might have disastrous results, that such a policy ' would strengthen the hands of the *Entente* and of internal counter-revolution.' These anarchists suggested that a commission of five persons, two of which were to be anarchists, should be appointed to go to Kronstadt and settle the dispute by peaceful means.

Naturally the Soviet Government paid no attention to this manifesto, and history has proven that, from the point of view of the Revolution, Emma Goldman's manifesto was wrong and the judgment of the Bolsheviki right. The suppression of the Kronstadt mutiny did not have disastrous results as far as the security of the Soviet Government was concerned. Morally, on the other hand, much can be said about the Government's policy during the mutiny, and this fact reflects the fundamental difference between the Bolsheviki and Emma Goldman. She, as a visionary and an idealist, judged situations and events from

180 SEVEN WOMEN AGAINST THE WORLD

a moral point of view, while the leading Bolsheviki were realists whose values were entirely practical and political.

It was obvious after Kronstadt that Emma Goldman was no longer a welcome guest in Soviet Russia. Berkman and she decided to leave. The Soviet Government did not arrest them ; the arrest of Emma Goldman, who had defended the Soviet Government during the early days of 1917 and 1918 would have made a very bad impression abroad, especially in the United States. Goldman and Berkman were given passports, and they left Russia late in November 1921.

They wandered from country to country ; no Government wanted to grant them a permit to stay. In Latvia they were allowed to remain for a short time ; then they went to Esthonia and to Sweden. Finally Emma Goldman was allowed to live in Germany. In Berlin she was relatively at peace. Her sister Stella came to stay with her, and an American publisher commissioned her to write her impressions of Russia. She remained in Germany until July 1924, when she came to England.

Never happy when she was not active, she hoped in England to ' rally the radical and Labour factions to the support of the political victims of the (Soviet) dictatorship.' Some of her friends felt, furthermore, that, as she says, ' her presence in England would be a stimulus to her own comrades.' Emma Goldman herself was not sure of her mission. ' I did not feel sanguine about the situation,' she writes ' I did not know how to reach the British people, and the only suggestion I could make was a dinner at some restaurant as my début before the London liberal public. My comrades were elated over the idea, and set to work.'

Her reception at this dinner was not entirely sympathetic. Many men and women among her

EMMA GOLDMAN 181

audience opposed her attack on Soviet Russia. When she began to discuss Russia in her after-dinner speech, 'shifting of chairs, turning of necks, and disapproval on the faces before her were the first indications that all was not going to be so harmonious as it seemed at first.'

Naturally, however, Emma Goldman continued her speech, and she did not give up her plan of winning British support for political prisoners in Russia. Some money was collected for a fund, but conditions in Russia were not affected by these efforts.

Actually, Emma Goldman had now become an observer. She was no longer able to take an active part in the social struggle. She married a Welsh miner, James Colton, and acquired British nationality, but there was no active work for a woman of her temperament to perform in England. She went to Canada, where she co-operated with anarchists in Toronto and other cities, but her work had become theoretical. The Communists naturally opposed or boycotted her meetings, and the majority of other Left Wing elements sided with them. This meant that she now had the radicals as well as the reactionaries against her. The success of Communism in Russia has made the doctrines of Anarchism more or less academic. The Governments of reactionary countries are no longer afraid of Anarchism, though they may fear the sporadic acts of individual anarchists. Emma Goldman was allowed to return to the United States on a visit, and her permanent home is in Canada. She herself is as optimistic, as undaunted, as she was twenty or thirty years ago, after so many disappointments her faith is unchanged.

'The fact that the Anarchist movement for which I have striven so long is to a certain extent in abeyance,' she wrote only last year, 'and is overshadowed by philosophies of authority and coercion, affect me with concern, but not with despair. It seems to me a

182 SEVEN WOMEN AGAINST THE WORLD

point of special significance that many countries decline to admit Anarchists. All governments hold the view that while parties of Right and Left may advocate social changes, still they cling to the idea of government and authority. Anarchism alone breaks with both and propagates uncompromising rebellion. In the long run, therefore, it is Anarchism which is considered deadlier to the present régime than all other social theories that are now clamouring for power.

'Considered from this angle I think that my life and my work have been successful. What is generally regarded as success—acquisition of wealth, the capture of power and social prestige—I consider the dismal failures. . . . I have always striven to remain in a state of flux and continued growth, and not to petrify in a niche of self-satisfaction. If I had my life to live over again, like any one else, I should wish to alter minor details, but in any of my more important actions and attitudes I would repeat my life as I have lived it. Certainly I should work for Anarchism with the same devotion and confidence in its ultimate triumph.'

VII

ROSA LUXEMBURG (1870–1919)

MANY of the revolutionary women of the nineteenth century were great and romantic figures whose heroic gestures inspired the masses, but none of them made a lasting contribution to revolutionary thought. In fact, it must be admitted that few of them thought clearly at all. Many of them were outstanding examples, but none of them were leaders, none of them were of international importance.

Rosa Luxemburg, the leader of the German *Spartakusbund* during the Great War, and the founder of the German Communist Party, was one of the first women whose mind, and whose actions, have left a permanent impression on the international revolutionary movement. She is generally acknowledged— by friends as well as enemies—to be one of the outstanding figures of our century, because—quite apart from the humanity she shared with earlier women revolutionaries—she combined a stupendous knowledge of economics with a keen imagination and a rare gift for action. She made original contributions to Socialist theory, but at the same time she fought in the front line of her movement. She founded the first German Communist newspaper, *Die Rote Fahne*, and was a brilliant journalist, but she never remained a passive observer. She was murdered by her opponents while on active service for her cause.

She was unusual also, because her knowledge and her contributions were not confined to the revolutionary movement of Germany, the country where she was killed. She was a Jewess, born in Poland, who knew Poland and Russia intimately ; she was

184 SEVEN WOMEN AGAINST THE WORLD

educated in Switzerland and in Paris, and she spent many years in Germany. She studied every problem before her from an international point of view; she was perfectly qualified to be a judge and a leader of the International Socialist movement.

Rosa Luxemburg was born on the 5th of March, 1870, in the town of Zamosc, in Russian Poland, but when she was three years old her parents moved to Warsaw, where she spent her childhood. Her father was a merchant who was greatly respected in Warsaw, and both he and her mother came of intellectual Jewish families. Russian and Polish were spoken in the home, but Eduard Luxemburg preferred the Polish language. He was one of those Polish Liberals who still hoped for Poland's independence, despite the fact that in the 'seventies and the 'eighties the Polish struggle for liberation from Russia was at its lowest ebb.

Rosa Luxemburg was a precocious, highly intelligent, and imaginative girl, the youngest of five children. Her physical disability—she was lame from some trouble in the hip—made her particularly sensitive. Besides, even as a grown woman, she was so small as to appear to be almost deformed. The fact that she never showed any self-consciousness about her physical disability, that she never allowed it to hamper her public career, reflects the insight and understanding her parents must have shown when she was a child.

Rosa Luxemburg was extremely young when she began to wonder about life, and there was a peculiarly mature undertone to her questions of why, wherefrom, or whereto. 'Life,' she wrote years later, during one of her terms in prison, 'seems always to be playing hide-and-seek with me. At home, I used to creep to the window early in the morning—we were not allowed to get up before my father had done so—and open it softly. Then I would gaze out onto the large court-yard. . . . At that time I was convinced that "Life," "real" life, was somewhere far away, over there

ROSA LUXEMBURG

beyond the roofs. Since then I have been pursuing life, but it always remains hidden behind some roofs.'

It reflected her lively temperament that as a child and a very young girl she was not satisfied merely to wonder about things. She wanted facts, not fancies, as answers to the questions which puzzled her. Almost from the time she could read she would spell out articles in the foreign Liberal newspapers which her father bought surreptitiously despite the rigid censorship then in force in Russian Poland. Just as some musical children begin early to pick out melodies on the piano, Rosa Luxemburg's young mind concentrated on political motives.

When she had gathered together the facts she wanted, furthermore, she was rarely content merely to let them sink into her consciousness. She longed to do something, to turn her thoughts and her emotions into action, into some expression. When she was eight years old she had the perseverance to express her grief at the death of her favourite canary in thirty sad verses.

By the time she was in her early teens she was not saddened only by helpless animals ; her attention was centred on the injustices suffered by men and women. She was fully aware of the oppression of the Tsarist régime in her own country, of the danger to human liberties of all monarchies on the continent of Europe. When she was fourteen, in 1884, the German Emperor, William I, made a state visit to Poland, and Rosa Luxemburg wrote a verse in Polish to him. 'For Emperor William's Arrival' it was called, and literally translated it said :

' Finally we shall see you, mighty man of the West,
That is to say I shall see you if you should come to the Saxon Garden,[1]
For I do not frequent your Courts.
For you must know that I care nothing for your honours.
But I should like to know what you gossip about at your Courts.

[1] The largest park in Warsaw.

186 SEVEN WOMEN AGAINST THE WORLD

I hear that you address our Tsar as a brother.
As far as politics are concerned I am still a stupid child,
So I do not want to discuss these things with you.
There is only one thing I should like to tell you, dear William:
Tell your sly cad of a Bismarck—
Do this for the sake of Europe, oh Emperor of the West—
Order him not to ruin the chances for peace.'

As this poem shows, Rosa Luxemburg was now keenly interested in politics, in the structure of society, in the characters of the men, such as Bismarck, who were controlling the destinies of Europe. Her brains and not her heart turned her into a Socialist, and this is the chief difference between her and the revolutionary women who came before her. ' I must have some one,' she wrote years later to Luise Kautsky, her great friend, ' who believes me when I say that I was plunged by chance into the whirlpool of world history and that I was really born to be a goose-girl.' Rosa Luxemburg's entire life, however, the fact that she never for an instant lost sight of her revolutionary aim, contradicts this passing mood.

She began to study the Socialist movement in Russia which until the late'eighties included the radical elements in Poland as well. While she was a pupil at the *Gymnasium*, the preparatory school at Warsaw, the first separate Socialist Polish organization, the *Proletariat*, was beginning to make itself felt. She read the books and speeches of the pioneers of this movement : Kunitzki, Ludwig Warynski, and S. Dickstein.

Rosa Luxemburg and some of her schoolfellows met secretly to talk about Socialism, to read Marx's *Communist Manifesto*, to discuss their hopes for the future. Unknown to the schoolmasters, they formed a small illegal club at the *Gymnasium*, and spread Socialist propaganda. Rosa Luxemburg had passed her matric—she had already been selected as the gold

ROSA LUXEMBURG 187

medallist of the *Gymnasium*—and was ready to go to the University by the time the police discovered these girls' subversive activities. Young as they were, however, the authorities would not have hesitated to arrest them, and Rosa Luxemburg was in grave danger, as she was the acknowledged leader of the group.

Naturally the Government refused her a passport, but her older friends in the Socialist movement decided that she should leave Poland at least for a time. They must have been quite aware of her outstanding ability, ability which later amounted to genius, for Martin Kaspschak, who was then at the head of the illegal Socialist activities in Warsaw, travelled with her to the frontier himself. It had been arranged that smugglers were to take her across the border, but the plan failed at the last moment. Kaspschak, therefore, went to the vicar in the frontier village and told him that the young Jewish girl with him wanted to leave Poland and go to Switzerland where she could be baptized and become a Christian. All effective revolutionaries, it seems, must be able, on occasion, to act a part, and Rosa Luxemburg had learned this lesson young. She assured the vicar that this was her reason for wanting to leave Poland, and he helped her across the frontier.

Rosa Luxemburg travelled to Zürich, where she matriculated at the University. She took a room in the home of a German Socialist refugee, Karl Lübeck, a chronic invalid, who supported himself by writing occasional articles for German Left Wing newspapers. His wife, who had been given the romantic name of Olympia, supplemented the tiny income by taking in the students' washing. The Lübecks were extremely kind to Rosa Luxemburg, and she in turn helped him with his articles. A few years later, when she decided to take an active part in the German Socialist movement, they arranged for

188 SEVEN WOMEN AGAINST THE WORLD

their son to enter into a formal marriage with her. She thus acquired German nationality and could not be deported from Germany. Naturally, this procedure annoyed the Germans, as it does all men, who strenuously object to the idea of women retaining their own nationality after marriage, and yet are grieved when some women turn the tables on them as Rosa Luxemburg did.

At the University of Zürich Rosa Luxemburg first matriculated in the philosophical faculty, but she soon changed her studies, specializing in political economy, economics, and law. She was entirely resolute in her intention of becoming a professional revolutionary, and knowledge seemed to her one of the most important weapons with which to fight the social battle.

Her reason for believing in knowledge as an essential factor in the coming class war was as clearly defined in her mind as was every other resolve she ever made. Rosa Luxemburg was never prompted by vague impulses.

' The end of the Paris Commune,' she declares in her famous *Junius Pamphlet* written in a Berlin prison during the Great War, ' closed the first stage of the European labour movement and the First International. Since then a new stage has begun. The spontaneous revolutions, revolts, and battles on the barricades, after which the proletariat relapsed into their former passivity, was replaced by a systematic day-to-day struggle, the exploitation of bourgeois parliamentarianism, the organization of the masses, the union of the economic and the political fight, and the Socialist ideal with the stubborn defence of the most obvious every day practical interests of the workers. For the first time the interests of the working classes and their emancipation was guided by strictly scientific teachings. The sects, schools of thought, utopias, and experiments which each country was following independently was replaced by a unified international

ROSA LUXEMBURG

theoretical basis, which held all countries together. Marx's insight supplied the working classes of the whole world with a compass which made it possible for them to see their way clearly through the whirlpool of current events, which made it possible for them hourly to direct the tactics of their struggle towards the immovable and final goal.'

Rosa Luxemburg's respect for hard cold facts, her faith in knowledge, however, never made her inhuman. It would be quite wrong to think of her merely as an outstanding brain. Her most severe economic writings include passages, written without pathos, which reflect her feeling for the working classes. In her doctor's thesis, for instance, crowded with statistics, she tells in simple words, but obviously moved by great pity, that in Moscow the workers in the factories were forbidden to sing while they worked. Five roubles were deducted from the wages of any man or woman who sang.

In Zürich, apart from her regular work at the University, Rosa Luxemburg began a strenuous course of self-education. She was training herself to a completely international point of view, and she made a systematic study of the labour movements of all European countries. This task was easier for her than it was for many others, for she was equally at home in Polish, Russian, German, or French, and she could read most other European languages as well.

While she was at the University she found time occasionally to contribute to various Socialist newspapers, and she thus first came into contact with Karl Kautsky, who was then editing the *Neue Zeit*, the new periodical of the German Social Democratic Party. Her correspondence with Kautsky reflects her quiet self-assurance. There is no arrogance of youth in her objective remarks about her own articles ; on the contrary, she had already acquired that modesty

190 SEVEN WOMEN AGAINST THE WORLD

of manner which usually comes only to people who have learned to accept success as a matter of course.

Even as a young student of politics Rosa Luxemburg was never narrow-minded. She was a woman of tremendous culture, if this word can still be used after the German Nazis have so consistently abused it for two years. She not only read books, she knew the literature of many countries. Her introduction to Korolenko's *History of my Times* reveals great knowledge of Russian literature. She was a sound and appreciative musician, people who have seen the portraits she painted say that she was a very competent artist. Later, when she had been in prison several times, she acquired a great understanding of the natural sciences, chiefly botany, which became her special hobby. The Russian revolutionaries were quite right when they called the Tsarist prisons ' the universities of the revolutionaries,' and later in Germany Rosa Luxemburg made excellent use of these somewhat unusual seats of learning.

Her intense intellectual interests never made her a recluse. At Zürich she associated with the other Polish and Russian students at the University. Most of them later joined the Polish Socialist Party, the ' P.S.P.,' which was founded in 1892. The members of this Party were not internationalists, but patriots, for they worked towards a liberation of Poland as well as for Socialism, or rather for social reforms.

Rosa Luxemburg sharply opposed those of her fellow students who defended this nationalist position, which to her seemed narrow and unrevolutionary. She called these nationalists ' social patriots.' As a result she was not liked by the Poles in Zürich, and her unpopularity was increased by the fact that she was so much cleverer than were her fellow-students. In his history of the Polish Socialist movement, Daczinski, who knew Rosa Luxemburg as a student,

ROSA LUXEMBURG

and who was later the Marshal of the Polish Sejm. attacks her bitterly for her ' quarrelsome ' nature.

In 1891 she met Leo Jogisches in Zürich, and he agreed with her about the future of the Socialist movement in Poland. They remained friends until they both died as victims of the Noske terror in Berlin in 1919, and together, as young people in Zürich, they laid the plans for the Social Democratic Party of Poland, which they founded in 1893 in strict opposition to the ' P.S.P.'

In 1893 Rosa Luxemburg also made her first appearance before the International Socialist Congress which met in Switzerland. Despite her youth—she was then only twenty-three—she made a profound impression on the older Socialists at the Congress ; she was accepted by most of them as their equal. Some of the men attending the Congress, however, were troubled by her severity ; it was obvious that this brilliant young woman would never waste her time on compromise. She would go straight for her aim, at no matter what cost. Every one at this Zürich meeting, however, must have realized that already she was ideally equipped for a revolutionary career. She had an original mind, she had courage, she was an excellent speaker, always quick at repartee, she knew what she wanted, yet she was always eager to learn. No personal interests or considerations or emotions would ever deter her. By temperament she was suited to live in the day, which after all is the only way for men and women who are constantly in danger to plan their lives. ' I do not believe in any long-term credits or obligations,' she once wrote.

She remained in Zürich until 1897 when, with a thesis on *The Industrial Development of Poland*, she took her doctor's degree in the faculty of law of the University. Then, resolved to work in Germany, she married Gustav Lübeck, a printer by trade. She arranged to be divorced immediately as he was an

192 SEVEN WOMEN AGAINST THE WORLD

anarchist, and she did not want to be associated even indirectly with the anarchist movement.

Her reasons for going to Germany were obvious. Since the defeat of the Paris Commune, as she herself once wrote, the European Labour movement had been centred in Germany. 'Just as France was the classic home of the first phase of the proletarian class struggle . . . the German working classes became the pioneers of the second stage of this struggle. At that time German Social-Democracy was not only the strongest advance guard, it was the thinking brain of the International.'

Before going to Germany Rosa Luxemburg spent some time in France completing her studies of the European labour movement. She frequently saw Jules Guesde, the editor of the *Droits de l'Homme*, and later of *Egalité*, who with Paul Lafargue, had tried to revive the French working-class movement after the defeat of the Commune. Rosa Luxemburg studied the activities of the *Parti Ouvrier Français*, which had been founded in the early 'eighties, and the *Possibilist Party*, the members of which believed in reform rather than in revolution. She also came into contact with the association of independent Socialists, founded in the early 'nineties, to which such men as Jaurés and Millerand belonged. The disunity amongst these various French groups must have presented an illuminating, though depressing, picture to Rosa Luxemburg's young and eager mind.

Rosa Luxemburg moved to Berlin in the spring of 1899. At this time German Socialists of the older, more radical, and more Marxian school of thought were quarrelling violently with the moderates, known as the ' Revisionists.' The unsurmountable differences between these two wings of the Socialist movement had became articulate at the first Congress held by the Social Democratic Party in Erfurt in the autumn of 1891. This was the first large public meeting of German Socialists after the repeal of Bismarck's harsh anti-Socialist laws.

Outwardly, of course, this Congress reflected the fact that German Socialism had been ultimately victorious in the struggle with Bismarck, that the working classes had won the right of political association. The *Erfurt Program*, furthermore, which had become famous in the history of Socialism, undoubtedly cleared away a great deal of confusion, of Utopian conceptions of the future. Lassalle's ideas of producers' unions, for instance, were officially recognized by the *Erfurt Program* to be impractical and useless.

Despite these achievements, however, the Erfurt Congress was not progressive, for the attitude of the Revisionists towards the future of the working classes showed that consciously or unconsciously they had been frightened and intimidated by the Iron Chancellor's ' Socialist Laws.' The Revisionists really gave up the idea of the class war and at heart they longed for a calm, classless society. In common with the vague emotional Socialists of the past, whom in their writings these Revisionists so bitterly attacked, they themselves harboured the illusion that the propertied classes would gradually be educated to sharing their possessions equally and fairly with the working classes. Actually the Revisionists were no longer Socialists, though they continued for more than twenty years to be known as such. These men had in effect become social reformers.

Eduard Bernstein, the leader of the Revisionists, asserted that the class war was quite unnecessary as ' in almost all Western countries the middle classes are no longer oppressing the Socialist movement ; at most the middle classes are on the defensive.' Accepting the temporary boom of German industry, due chiefly to her colonial expansion, as a permanent condition, and evading any consideration of the future,

194 SEVEN WOMEN AGAINST THE WORLD

Bernstein also claimed that the working classes were no longer impoverished ; on the contrary, he asserted they were becoming increasingly prosperous. He was convinced that the propertied classes were politically progressive and fair-minded.

Bernstein observed furthermore that ' the big industrial capitalists are swallowing up the very small enterprises, but not by any means the moderately large concerns. The latter on the contrary,' he declared, ' comprise an increasing number of small capitalists.' He deduced from this fact that, contrary to the prophecies of Marx, surplus values were not coming increasingly into the control of a few powerful capitalists. Bernstein believed, on the contrary, that these surplus values would gradually come into the hands of a wider section of the population and that eventually the working classes would be given their share. As the industrial development of the last forty years has shown, Bernstein and his friends were entirely wrong in this assumption, which for them was one of the reasons for giving up the class war.

' Social democracy,' Bernstein had declared at the Erfurt Congress, ' should neither expect nor desire the break-up of the present economic system. Its task for many years to come is politically to organize the working classes, to prepare them for democracy and for reforms within the State, and these reforms are calculated to raise the living standards of the workers.'

Naturally Rosa Luxemburg, who was always a realist, strenuously opposed the Revisionists, whose misguided ideas directed the German Social Democratic Party until its solution when the Nazi régime came into power in 1933. In her fight against the Revisionists—and her great talents as a journalist were already recognized by her friends and by her enemies —she was closely associated with August Bebel, Wilhelm Liebknecht, and Karl Kautsky, who was at this time opposing the Revisionists' doctrines of which he later approved.

In two series of articles in the *Leipziger Volkszeitung*, one published before and one after she came to Germany, Rosa Luxemburg attacked and refuted the Revisionists' theories. ' Fourier's idea,' she writes in one of these articles which were later published in a pamphlet called *Social Reform or Revolution*, ' of suddenly changing all the sea water in the world into lemonade with the help of the Phalanstere System, was very fantastic. Bernstein's idea, on the other hand, of changing the capitalist sea of bitterness into a sea of socialist sweetness by adding Socialist-reforming lemonade into this sea bottle by bottle, is merely more insipid but no less fantastic than Fourier's ideas.'

After this outburst against Bernstein, Rosa Luxemburg goes on to say—and this paragraph might be the credo of any modern Socialist : ' Conditions of production in capitalist society are increasingly approaching Socialist conditions of production. The political and judicial conditions of capitalist society on the other hand, are erecting an increasingly high wall between Capitalism and Socialism. The wall is not broken through either by the development of social reforms or by democracy. On the contrary, special reforms of democracy will only strengthen this wall and make it more unsurmountable. This wall can be torn down only by the hammering of the revolution—that is to say, by the capture of political power by the working classes.'

Rosa Luxemburg had become an active factor in the German Socialist movement. She joined the staff of the *Vorwärts*, the daily Socialist paper in Berlin. She associated chiefly, of course, with the members of that wing of the Party which opposed the Revisionists. She moved to a small flat in Friedenau, on the western outskirts of Berlin, so that

196 SEVEN WOMEN AGAINST THE WORLD

she could be near Karl and Luise Kautsky, who were soon her closest personal friends. When the Kautskys went away, Rosa Luxemburg stayed in their flat to look after their boys. Despite her later differences with Kautsky, who was increasingly drawn into the Revisionists' camp, her friendship for Luise Kautsky persisted.

In January 1904 Rosa Luxemburg went to prison for *lèse majesté*. She spent several months in the women's prison at Zwickau, in Saxony, but she was amnestied when Frederick Augustus of Saxony came to the throne.

That year she also came into contact with Lenin for the first time. In an article in the *Neue Zeit* she criticized the rigid methods of organization carried through by Lenin and the other Russian *émigrés* living in Switzerland ; she objected to their seclusion, and considered it a mistake that they kept themselves aloof from the masses in Russia.

Defenders of Lenin's policy point out, and perhaps quite rightly, as M. Philips Price says, that Rosa Luxemburg's ' warning was well timed, especially for the Socialists in Western and Central Europe, who were not living under the same conditions as the Russians, and who were able to carry on legal propaganda among the masses. The Russian revolutionaries, on the other hand, were justified, under the circumstances prevailing in their country at the time, in following their line of tactics. Measures of a stringent nature had to be taken to prevent *agents provocateurs* and spies of the Tsarist régime from getting into the Party, since the Party was illegal, and work had to be carried on underground.'

Rosa Luxemburg's heated controversy with Lenin is not of historical importance, except that it is quoted again and again by Social-Democrats to prove that she disagreed fundamentally with Lenin. For a curious struggle had been going on between members of the Second and quite logically the Third International about her : both admit that she was one of the greatest minds of the Socialist movement, and both therefore want to claim her as one of their own. Some German Social Democrats assert in this connection, and probably wrongly, that she would have become less extreme had she lived to witness the developments of the German Republic.

In her pamphlet on the *Russian Revolution*, published by Paul Levi after her death, and written in a Berlin prison where, it should be mentioned, she was cut off from up-to-date news of the Revolution of 1917, she does indeed criticize some of Lenin's tactics. In this pamphlet, however, she clearly states that to Lenin and his Party ' are due the eternal historical achievement of proclaiming for the first time the goal of Socialism as the direct programme of practical politics.' (' Sie haben sich damit den unvergaenglichen geschichtlichen Verdienst erworben, zum ersten Mal die Endziele des Sozialismus als unmittelbares Programm der praktischen Politik zu proklamieren.')

Just as, had she lived, she would undoubtedly have supported the main achievement of the Russian Revolution, she would, equally, have kept aloof from that religious reverence which so many Communists feel for Lenin. She would have remained as critical of him, and as objective about his government, as she was in 1904, when in a letter to Frau Kautsky she impatiently referred to something that Lenin had said as the ' Babblings of Ulianoff ' (' Quasselei des Ulianoff ').

It was only natural that Rosa Luxemburg was more deeply concerned with Lenin and his programme than were other German Socialists. For she followed the Polish revolutionary movement as closely as she had done as a student in Zürich, and everything which happened in Russia or Poland interested her profoundly. In the autumn of 1905 she gave up her

198 SEVEN WOMEN AGAINST THE WORLD

post at the *Vorwärts* and left Berlin for Poland. She went to take part in the illegal revolutionary movement, and she took with her a false passport made out to ' Anna Matschke.'

She was extremely active both in Warsaw and in Moscow organizing the revolt of the workers, writing and printing leaflets, calling on the men and women employed in the factories to join the revolution, arranging secret meetings. She showed that many years of more or less theoretical work in German Socialism had by no means dulled her ability as an active revolutionary.

In March 1906 the Russian Police discovered that Rosa Luxemburg and Leo Jogisches, with whom she had been co-operating closely, were largely responsible for the revolutionary upheaval in Poland. They were both arrested, and he was sentenced to eight years banishment in Siberia. He escaped from the Warsaw prison where he was detained before he was to be deported to Siberia and continued his work in Warsaw. Rosa Luxemburg, too, was able to escape ; German Socialists had provided the money with which to bribe the warders of the Polish prison-fortress. She fled to Finland, where she rested for a few weeks before returning to Germany.

Conditions in the fortress-prison in Warsaw where Rosa Luxemburg had been detained were horrible. When the prisoners were allowed to receive a visitor they were locked in an iron cage. This cage was then surrounded by an iron grating so that the caged prisoner and the visiting relative were several feet apart. Rosa Luxemburg remembered that once when her brother came to see her she was hardly able to stand. She had been on hunger strike for six days and was too weak to walk from her cell to the cage. One of the prison officials carried her there and placed her into the cage, but no chair was given her, and she clung to the iron bars to prevent herself from falling. When one remembers how frail she was at the best of times, it shows her gallant sense of humour when she asked her brother whether she did not remind him of a wild animal at the Zoo.

Her activities during her illegal visit to Poland and Russia were typical of the manner in which she attacked any problem. She had worked feverishly on the problems arising from day to day in connection with the Revolution ; no routine task was too humble for her to undertake ; she was her own editor, printer, and, if necessary, errand boy. Yet, simultaneously, her mind was busy registering her experiences, analysing the situation, pointing out mistakes which had been made, deducing what lessons revolutionaries in Western Europe could learn from the Russian Revolution of 1905.

When she was in Finland she reconsidered everything that had happened, she reconstructed the events of 1905 step by step in her imagination. And she came to the conclusion that Western European Socialists must again accept the idea of the mass strike as the most important factor in any revolution. Sporadic revolts, she concluded, were useless ; only the support of the masses would finally achieve the Revolution. Her pamphlet on this subject *Massenstreik, Partei und Gewerkschaften*—for it was typical of her that she at once wrote down her conclusions—was published in Hamburg that year.

Nowadays, makers of revolutions, or would-be makers of them, take the general strike into account. Early in the century, however, when Socialists clung to Marx's and Engels' every utterance, the attitude towards this method was different. The early Socialists had considered a mass strike an entirely impractical suggestion made by impractical anarchists such as Bakunin. Friedrich Engels, for instance, who attacked Bakunin's ideas in 1873, argued that if the working classes were ever rich and powerful enough to organize

200 SEVEN WOMEN AGAINST THE WORLD

a general strike in the event of a revolution, they would already be in control of the situation and a strike would no longer be necessary.

In her pamphlet Rosa Luxemburg tried to make the workers in Western European countries realize that Engels' point of view no longer held good. 'The Russian Revolution,' she wrote, 'has made it necessary to revise our judgement of his (Engels') arguments. For the first time in history, in this Revolution, the idea of the strike of the masses and of the general strike has been magnificently carried out. Thus a new epoch in the development of the labour movement has begun.' She then continues with a detailed analysis of the application of the strike as it occurred in Russia.

Though many of the older and more influential German Socialists, including Kautsky, fundamentally disagreed with her belief that the working classes should be educated to mass action, there were as yet no signs of the bitter disagreements which were to separate her from the Social Democratic Party in a few years. When she returned to Germany from Finland she was appointed as instructor of economics at the School for Officials of the Party, and her former pupils say that she was a brilliant teacher. She wrote an economic text-book *Einführung in die Nationalöko-nomie*, and in 1912 she published her most famous book, *The Accumulation of Capital*, which is believed by many theoretical Socialists to supplement Marx in a way which will make it have an increasing influence.

The possibility of war was widely discussed on the Continent for several years before 1914, and Rosa Luxemburg never for an instant ignored this terrible possibility, either in her public speeches or her writings. In 1908, at the International Socialist Congress held at Stuttgart in South Germany she, with August Bebel, Lenin, and Martoff, put through a resolution ' against war and imperialism.' This resolution stated ' that the fight against militarism could no longer be separated from the class struggle as a whole. . . . War between capitalist states are as a rule the result of their competition for world markets.' The Congress therefore resolved that should war break out despite the efforts of the working classes to prevent it, it was their duty and that of their representatives in parliaments to do everything in their power, to apply any means whatsoever which would seem effective to stop it. Should a war break out, this Congress decided, ' It is the duty of all Socialists to do what they can to end the hostilities quickly ; they must furthermore make use of the economic and political crisis resulting from the war to agitate the people thus hastening the downfall of the capitalist system.'

Months before the Great War began, in lectures on ' the political and economic situation and the duties of the working classes,' Rosa Luxemburg was urging German workers to decline to fight, to unite in mass action against war, to work for peace. She was arrested after a meeting in the small town of Sachsenhausen, and accused of ' suggesting a mass strike to the people, agitating for murder, and instigating to mutiny.' At her trial on September 26, 1913, she asked the prosecuting attorney why he used the word ' mutiny ' as, after all, no war was in progress.' She added, however, that if she had been addressing an audience of soldiers, she would not have altered one single word of her speech. She was sentenced to one year's imprisonment, but she was not called upon to serve this sentence until early in 1915.

The outbreak of the War was a terrible shock for Rosa Luxemburg. At that time there were 110 Social Democratic members in the German Reichstag. In the party meeting before the Reichstag session, 14 of these members had voted against the War, but

202 SEVEN WOMEN AGAINST THE WORLD

when the vital question came to the vote in the Parliament all of them ' maintained the Party discipline ' and voted for the War. Karl Liebknecht, too, who with Rosa Luxemburg later became the most aggressive anti-war agitator in Germany, on that day accepted the opinion of the majority of his Party.

The masses, too, were largely in favour of their leaders' decision for, as was the case in every country, the German workers were told that this was a war of defence, that the enemy was the aggressive factor in the struggle. Besides, the German workers, since the days of Marx, had been in terror of a Russian invasion, a Russian victory which might introduce Tsarist absolutism into Germany.

Rosa Luxemburg, who always saw decades ahead of her contemporaries, and who undoubtedly would not have been in the least surprised had she seen the disastrous results of the War in our own day, twenty years later, was beside herself at the action taken by the German Socialist leaders ; at the attitude of the masses. For her Social Democracy had failed now that it was put to the test of a real crisis. She realized that, in this crisis, the international union of the working classes had been ineffectual. The international resolutions about the workers' duty in time of war had been empty talk. The leaders, and many of the workers themselves, had changed from theoretical internationalists into patriots, defending the property and interests of the capitalist class.

In the German *Official Handbook for Social Democratic Voters* for 1911, as Rosa Luxemburg herself bitterly recalls in her *Junius Pamphlet*, the leaders of the German Party had written : ' Do our rulers and our governing classes believe that the peoples of the world would ever take part in such a monstrous act ? Will not a cry of horror, anger, and indignation rise from the peoples and cause them to end this murder ? Will they not ask : For whom are we fighting ? What is this carnage for ? Are we mad to be treated like this or to submit to being treated like this ? Any one quietly contemplating the possibility of a great European war can only come to these conclusions.'

A week before the declaration of war, on July 26, 1914, the German Socialist Press still published articles in the following vein : ' We are not marionettes. We shall fight with every ounce of energy a system which turns human beings into mere tools of a situation which rules blindly ; we shall fight Capitalism, which is trying to change Europe, thirsting for peace, into a slaughter-house.'

By August 4, such bold statements had ceased, and Rosa Luxemburg went through that ghastly experience of observing that the men and women in whom she had believed for so long were betraying Socialism.

' For a few days,' Karl Radek describes her frame of mind after war was declared, ' Rosa Luxemburg was overcome by wild despair. Her friends were extremely anxious about her, as she had serious heart trouble. But she pulled herself together at once, and was one of the first to begin the fight against this treachery. She travelled all over Germany, trying to gather up loose threads and getting information which would help her to understand the possibilities of the situation. Soon, too, she began her fight against the ensnaring phrases which the Government Socialists were using to confuse the masses, though the only paper open to her at the time was a little party newspaper in Gotha.'

During the War Rosa Luxemburg spent altogether three years and four months in prison, partly in the Women's Prison in the Barnim Strasse in Berlin, the prison where so many socialist, pacifist, and liberal women have been detained since the beginning of the Nazi régime, and partly in the Women's Prison in Breslau, in Silesia. She was extremely active mentally,

204 SEVEN WOMEN AGAINST THE WORLD

and as a writer, while she was cut off from the hopeless struggle her associates were waging against the World War.

She had time to think about the War, and not only to feel outraged regret about it. ' One thing is certain,' she wrote in 1915, ' the World War marks the beginning of a new epoch in world history. It would be folly to believe that we need only survive it in order, after it is over, to resume life at its former pace—like a hare awaiting the end of a storm under a bush. The World War has altered the conditions of our [the Socialists'] fight, and it has changed us most of all. This does not mean that the basis of capitalist development, and the war unto death between capital and labour, has changed or became less bitter. . . . Historically this War will greatly further the interests of the proletariat.'

In her *Junius Pamphlet*, which she called the *Crisis of Social Democracy*, she analysed the fatal mistakes made by the Social Democratic Party in Germany. To her, and to many others in that country, it was already becoming obvious that from the point of view of the social revolution this Party was finished, an institution of the past. Rosa Luxemburg's *Spartakusbund* (the Spartacus Association), for the members of which she wrote many ' letters ' which were smuggled out of prison, included a number of revolutionary socialists who had left the old Social Democratic Party. This *Spartakusbund*, to which, apart from Luxemburg, such men as Karl Liebknecht, Leo Yogisches, who was then in Germany, and Franz Mehring belonged, was the forerunner of the German Communist Party, founded by Rosa Luxemburg late in 1918.

In the spring of 1917 another radical group broke away from the Social Democratic Party. These men, known as the Independent Socialist Party, began actively to oppose the War. In 1917 and until late in 1918 the *Spartakusbund* functioned as the radical wing of the Independent Socialist Party. A number of the Spartacists believed that these two groups should be definitely separated, but Rosa Luxemburg insisted that they must work together.

' The Independent Socialist Party and the *Spartakusbund,*' she wrote, ' are two complementary heirs to the inheritance of German and international Social Democracy ; the former representing the practical experience of the old movement, and the latter the theoretical outlook of the future. Hence the sharp opposition between these two groups, an opposition which embodies at once the tragic, internal conflict of the working class movement. This conflict cannot, however, be solved mechanically by separating the two organizations. It can only be solved in the open, by a constant and systematic struggle between the two groups within one and the same Party, and in the long-run it can only be decided by objective historical developments.'

Political considerations of this kind were not the only interests which occupied Rosa Luxemburg during her imprisonment. She translated Korolenko into German, and her letters to Sonja Liebknecht, Karl Liebknecht's wife, to whom she was deeply attached, reflect her growing interest in natural sciences. These letters were full of the botanical discoveries she made —from books and not from gardens—in her cell. From the window, and when she was allowed to go out into the prison courtyard or the small prison garden, she watched and observed birds, beetles, any living creatures she could see.

At times—and all public characters must experience this longing—she wished fervently that she could have, or could have had, more energy and leisure for her private life. ' Temperamentally,' she once wrote to Sonja Liebknecht, ' I feel more at home in this tiny garden or in a field than I do at—a Party Congress.

206 SEVEN WOMEN AGAINST THE WORLD

I can tell you this quite frankly : you will not jump to the conclusion that I am betraying Socialism when I feel like this. You know that despite this feeling I shall die at my post : in a street battle or in prison. But my real self belongs more to my birds than to my " comrades." '

In March 1916, when one of her prison sentences came to an end, she was again at liberty for about a year. Early in 1917 she frequently saw Karl Lieb-knecht, who had been called up for active service, but was at home on leave. Liebknecht and Luxemburg made an attempt to call together a May Day demonstration in the Potsdamer Platz in Berlin. A small but courageous crowd came to support this anti-war gathering, and Liebknecht, himself wearing the field-grey uniform of the simple soldier, shouted at the top of his lungs : ' Down with the War.' This gallant gesture must have encouraged many timid souls who approved the meeting, but who had not dared to come to the Potsdamer Platz, and five thousand workers in armament plants attempted to strike.

Liebknecht was arrested at once, but for some curious reason Rosa Luxemburg was not sent back to prison for two months. Then she had a very bad time. From his own fortress-prison Karl Liebknecht wrote to his wife about Luxemburg's arrest : ' I hear that my friend, Rosa Luxemburg, was arrested on July 10 (1918),' he writes, '. . . she is delivered up to her enemies, and her frail health will suffer terribly in the bad air, as she can have no exercise out of doors. Last February she was dragged off in the " green cart " with whores and women thieves ; then she was in prison for a year. Now they want to destroy her entirely, they want to destroy this woman, whose frail body carries such a glowing, such a great soul, such a daring, brilliant mind. She will have lasting fame in the history of human civilization, long after the 42-centimetre heroes of military barbarism are held in contempt or forgotten.' Liebknecht closes this letter with these words : ' The force which they would like to conquer by conquering Rosa Luxemburg is stronger than the law of " right is might " which prevails in this state of siege. This force will burst the walls of her prison and will triumph.'

Liebknecht's anxiety about Rosa Luxemburg was justified. Her health, never very good, had suffered noticeably and she had been shocked by the death at the front of Hans Dieffenbach, one of her greatest friends, who had fallen late in 1917. ' I cannot overcome my profound astonishment,' she wrote shortly after his death to Luise Kautsky ; ' is this possible ? It is like a word which has become silent in the middle of a sentence, like a chord which is suddenly stopped, and which I can hear no longer. . . . I cannot grasp it yet : is this possible ? It is like a flower which has been torn off its stem and is trampled upon. . . .'

There were moments, though only moments, during her last prison sentence, when she almost lost her nerve, when the terrible strain of the war began to tell upon her.

' Do you know,' she once wrote to Frau Kautsky, ' what thought is persecuting and frightening me ? I imagine that I must go into a huge hall, crowded with people, that the glaring lights, the buzzing talk of the crowd press down upon me, that the usual tumultuous applause greets me as I make my way to the platform—then I suddenly feel that I shall run away, I have what is known as *horror pleni*, and even the thought of sitting with five or six friends, and perhaps hearing loud laughter, frightens me.'

On the 9th of November 1918, when the German Republic was proclaimed, the prison doors were opened and political prisoners found themselves suddenly at liberty. Rosa Luxemburg was hurled from the oppressive solitude of her cell into a huge mass demonstration in the Cathedral Square in Breslau.

208 SEVEN WOMEN AGAINST THE WORLD

Her absolute poise, her outward calm, and her forceful speech on this occasion reflect not only her self-control, but her vitality, her complete devotion to a cause which made her entirely forget her own nervous exhaustion.

On the 10th of November the Assembly of representatives of the Soldiers' and Workers' Council met in the Circus Busch in Berlin and elected the new Republican Government of Germany. The Independent Socialist Party agreed to form a coalition government with the Social Democratic Party, now usually known as the Majority Socialists, and at the Circus Busch meeting each Party put up three People's Representatives. This Provisional Government, consisting of these six men, was to govern the new Republic until the Constituent Assembly elected a permanent Government. The rebellious soldiers and sailors of the former Imperial Army brought about the German Revolution, but the authority in the new State was taken over by the moderate Majority Socialists, who did not really believe in the social revolution, who wanted 'law and order,' who were, in fact, exceedingly nervous of any startling upheaval.

On November 10, 1918, when the soldiers and sailors had infected large sections of the population with revolutionary fervour, an article published in the *Vorwärts*, the official organ of the Social Democratic Party, showed to what an extent the old Revisionists' conservatism had by now penetrated the Party. 'Citizens,' the *Vorwärts* wrote, 'keep off the streets; keep law and order,' and two days before, this paper had warned German Socialists not to act without thinking (' keine Unbesonnenheit ').

As the attitude of the Majority Socialists shows, the German ' Revolution ' of 1918 was not a socialist revolution. ' As a whole, after November tenth,' as Professor Rosenberg points out in his excellent study

of the German Republic, ' Germany as a political
unit remained what it had been in October of that
same year : a bourgeois-democratic state.'
The German ' Revolution,' unlike other revolutions in history, was actually the result of a military
defeat ; it did not spring from an organized and
popular socialist action against a government in
power. The German ' Revolution ' was prompted
largely by a negative force : the people's weariness
of war and defeat in war, rather than by a positive
concentrated effort to change the existing order.
It was historically only logical, therefore, that no
attempt was made to reorganize the administration
of the new Germany on socialist lines. The Emperor
and the rulers of the small German dynasties had been
removed, but the civil service was not revolutionized.
True, Social Democratic ministers were included in
the Republican Cabinets, but the most important
institutions in the State remained practically unchanged. The Judicial system, above all, was not
vitally affected by the Republican régime ; the judges
of the old Germany remained in office. That is how
it was possible, while the German Republic lasted,
that so many men, who became National Socialists
and later destroyed this Republic, could have been
acquitted even after their Movement was recognized
as a great danger to the State.
Almost immediately after the proclamation of the
Republic, furthermore, Noske, the Social Democratic
Minister of War, associated himself with officers of
the old Imperial Army to bring about the downfall
of those Socialists, such as Rosa Luxemburg, who still
believed in Socialism. This connexion between the
Republican Government and the officers of the old
Army encouraged them in the formation of those
military associations, beginning with the *Freikorps*,
which in due course attacked the Republic. These
associations were the nucleus of the private army finally

organized by the National Socialists to overthrow the Republic.

The big industrialists, of course, welcomed the moderate tactics adopted by the rulers of the new Germany. ' They were willing to agree to anything,' as Professor Rosenberg writes, ' as long as they could remain in control of their property. They promised to recognize the trades unions, to accept the eight-hour day, they were willing to go into the matter of wage demands and a fundamental reorganization of working conditions in the factories. They were willing to co-operate with the workers' organizations, to discuss and settle all questions concerning industry with the leaders of the trades unions, if only, by so doing, they could escape expropriation.'

As a whole the German working class was willing and eager to accept these new working conditions which interested them more keenly than a vague hope of a future Socialist State. They were exhausted from four years of war, from the blockade, from hunger. No one can deny that the Majority Socialists repre-sented the wishes of the moment of the majority of the people when they stood for ' law and order.'

It was equally true, however, that the radical element of the population was roused to even greater dis-content when they realized that the German ' Revolu-tion ' was in no way to mean an overthrow of the capitalist system. The Independent Socialists in the Provisional Government tried in vain to counteract the policy of the Majority Socialists.

The Independents were particularly incensed when the Provisional Government fraternized with the officers of the old Army in order to overcome the resistance of the revolutionary element in the masses. The First All-German Congress of Workers' and Sailors' Councils, which met in Hamburg in December 1918, had put forward a plan for the organization of a republican militia. The most important of the

'Hamburg decisions' reached by this Congress provided that the army should henceforth be completely in the control of the people's commissioners, thus removing the Imperial officers from positions of influence. When, in December, the Majority Socialists refused to accept the 'Hamburg decisions' and continued to support the old Army leaders, the Independent Socialists resigned from the Provisional Government.

This meant that the struggle between the Majority Socialists and the Socialists who interpreted the word 'socialism' to mean a control of the State by the working classes had come out into the open. In his *Aus der Werkstatt der Deutschen Revolution*, Emil Eichorn, an Independent Socialist who was the Police President of Berlin at the time, summarizes this situation :

'The differences were not based on superficial issues. They were rooted in our different interpretation of the November Revolution. I regarded the achievements of November the ninth as not yet carried to their logical conclusion ; I was in favour of a further development of the Revolution in the direction of Socialism. Wels [one of the Majority Socialist leaders] regarded the Revolution as finished with the entry of the Majority Socialists into the Government and into the higher departments of State.'

Rosa Luxemburg and Karl Liebknecht naturally agreed that the November Revolution had remained incomplete, but the isolated years she had spent in prison had not shaken her realism. She had no more illusions about the German working classes than she had about the Majority Socialists and the unsocialist nature of the November Revolution. The fact that millions of German workers, who had been members of the Social Democratic Party for years, had supported the War enthusiastically in 1914, showed her clearly that nothing could be gained by a *coup d'état*, that it would take years to educate the

212 SEVEN WOMEN AGAINST THE WORLD

masses of the people to a really Socialist outlook. Her belief in the necessity of mass action had not altered.

As the leader of the *Spartakusbund* she emphasized this point of view on December 30, 1918, when the Spartacists officially separated from the Independent Socialists and became the Communist Party of Germany. In her address at the first Party Congress she declared :

' The *Spartakusbund* will never take over power, except with the clear, unanimous will of the majority of the proletarian masses of Germany and unless they consciously agree with the opinions, the aims, and the methods adopted by the *Spartakusbund*.

' The proletarian revolution can only develop clearly and soundly if it develops gradually, step by step on a Golgotha path of our own bitter experiences and through victories and defeats. The victory of the *Spartakusbund* is not at the beginning but at the end of the Revolution. Our victory is identical with the victory of the large masses, including millions, of the socialist proletariat.'

As this admonition to her fellow-Spartacists shows, Rosa Luxemburg, unlike most of the men in her audience at this first Congress of the German Communist Party, was not for an instant carried away by the success of the Russian Revolution. She never forgot that conditions in Germany were entirely different from those prevailing in Russia when the Revolution broke out.

' Comrades,' she called out to her excited listeners, many of whom were angered by her insistence that they desist from a revolt, ' Comrades, you take your radicalism rather too easily. Despite the stress and the urgency of the moment we must not lose our ability seriously to contemplate the situation. When the National Assembly was forcefully dismissed in Russia, the Government of Trotski and Lenin already existed. We are still governed by Ebert and Scheidemann. The Russian Proletariat had been through a long epoch of revolutionary struggles. We in Germany are only at the beginning of our Revolution. We have experienced nothing but the miserable half-revolution of the ninth of November. So we must ask ourselves which is the surest way for us to educate the masses.'

Luxemburg and Liebknecht wanted to begin this education, to launch the ' step-by-step ' revolution, by sending representatives of the new Communist Party into the National Assembly and later into the new Reichstag. This suggestion, tragically enough for Liebknecht and Luxemburg, was voted down at the Congress. Only twenty-three delegates remained clear-sighted enough to vote for Luxemburg's proposal ; sixty-two delegates who believed in immediate revolutionary action voted against her.

What happened in January 1919 was only the logical historical outcome of this decision. The Spartacist rising in Berlin in January 1919 was doomed to failure. The Majority Socialist Government easily suppressed this rebellion with the help of the Imperial troops, who were filled with violent hatred against the Spartacists.

The Majority Socialists were, of course, made uneasy by the radical Berlin Workmen's Council, which was a constant danger to the new State. The Majority Socialist Government therefore dismissed Emil Eichhorn and appointed a less radical Police President. The Spartacists, joined by a number of Independent Socialists, then organized a revolt in Berlin, occupied the offices of the *Vorwärts*, and issued a proclamation declaring that the Ebert-Scheidemann Government had been deposed. Naturally it was an easy matter for the well-armed Majority Socialist troops to quell this revolt in a few days.

Rosa Luxemburg was in a most tragic situation. She had never doubted that such sporadic revolts

214 SEVEN WOMEN AGAINST THE WORLD

would be futile. She must have known that if she remained in Berlin, she, as leader of the Spartacists, would inevitably be brought to trial or executed; she knew that she would suffer for an uprising which she had opposed. And yet she could not bring herself to desert her fellow-Spartacists in this inevitable defeat.

She remained in Berlin, where, any day, Noske or his associates would arrest her. She spent most of her time encouraging the defeated rebels in the columns of *Die Rote Fahne*, the new Communist newspaper.

'. . . this struggle in the German revolution,' she wrote about the January rising, ' has ended in defeat. But the Revolution is a form of war, in which the final victory is only brought about by a series of defeats. For what does the history of modern Revolutions show us ? The whole road of Socialism is strewn with defeats. And the same road leads step by step to final victory. Where should we be without the defeats from which we gather historical knowledge ? To-day, on the eve of the last decisive struggle, we have come to that defeat which we must all experience, which is a part of our education. So far, revolutions have brought us only defeats, but these defeats carry with them the guarantee of our future victory. But only under one condition, and that is, if we really understand the circumstances which brought about our defeat. . . . The masses are the decisive factor ; they are the field on which the final victory of the Revolution will be attained. It is the masses who have made this " defeat " one in the chain of historic defeats, which are at once the pride and the power of the international socialist movement.'

By the middle of January, Liebknecht and Luxemburg were in great personal danger, as Noske had ordered the homes of any persons suspected of being connected with the January rising to be searched.

ROSA LUXEMBURG

Their friends finally persuaded Luxemburg and Lieb-knecht to leave their own flats and to stay with friends in Wilmersdorf, in the west end of Berlin.

Officers of a *Freikorps*, one of the organizations of ex-officers of the old Army, who were helping the Majority Socialists to down the rising, discovered the hiding-place of Liebknecht and Luxemburg. They were taken in a car to the Eden Hotel, which these officers used as their headquarters. Rosa Luxem-burg's friends have always hoped that she did not know she was going to be killed, for she took a suitcase with her, and she may have thought that she was merely on her way to prison, or at least to a decent trial.

She and Liebknecht were conducted to a room in the Eden Hotel where they were questioned by three officers—Vogel, Pflug Hartungk, and Krull. Then Rosa Luxemburg was brought down again. As she was leaving the hotel, and her limp always made her walk slowly, Runge, one of the soldiers whose prisoner she was, stepped up behind her and struck her down with the end of his heavy gun. She was carried to a waiting car. The officers who had questioned her got into it and drove off. Runge, who later confessed his part in this terrible murder, reported that then, when Rosa Luxemburg stirred—either consciously or unconsciously—Lieutenant Krull put his revolver to her head and shot her. Her body was then flung into the canal.

The Majority Socialists had bitterly attacked Rosa Luxemburg the day before in the *Vorwärts*: ' Viel Hundert Tote in einer Reih, Karl, Rosa, Radek und Kumpanei, es ist keiner dabei.' The Government now supported her murderers by allowing them to be tried by a court-martial consisting of their fellow-officers. Naturally they were acquitted. As R. T. Clark points out in his remarkable study of the *Fall of the German Republic*, to condone this murder ' was to the eternal

216 SEVEN WOMEN AGAINST THE WORLD

shame ' of the Majority Socialist Government of the new German Republic.

It will take years for the revolutionary movement in Germany to recover from the loss of Rosa Luxemburg. Her death presents one of the most tragic ' ifs ' of modern history. If she had lived might not the development of Germany have been less disastrous ? These considerations are all the more tragic as she might so easily have lived to form a more united Socialist opposition to the rising Hitler movement.

For her to have left Berlin would have meant desertion. She could not go. And only she had the right to decide this question which for herself involved life or death. Historically, however, it has become quite clear that her sacrifice was too great ; she was desperately missed in Germany after her death. The Majority Socialists would have been more constantly reminded by her presence of the Socialism they had, in practice, abandoned, and her own Party, the Communist, would have been prevented by her from making many of the mistakes they made after her death.

VIII

IS THERE A REVOLUTIONARY TYPE?

THE ways of history are always difficult to understand ; and as far as women are concerned these ways have been particularly erratic ; there seems to be no logical sequence of cause and effect, of efforts and achievements. Perhaps this has been so because men, who for centuries directed the destinies of women, have not always been consistent in their attitude towards them.

In Catholic countries, for instance, where men worship one woman as divine, women have not attained their civic rights, and they had not done so even before many of these countries became Fascist and therefore naturally anti-feminist. Yet, in Protestant countries, where the deities are male, men have been more enlightened, and women's position has been more favourable.

In France, which produced more great political revolutionary women than any other European country, women have not yet got the vote, but nevertheless they have a very far-reaching economic influence, especially among the *petit-bourgeoisie*, where the prejudice against women in politics is more general than it is in any other class of society. Perhaps the French tradition of women's indirect rule, established by such women as Madame de Maintenon or Madame de Pompadour, and strengthened by women's political *salons*, has been so strong that it persists in the French mentality. Perhaps some Frenchwomen themselves prefer to be the invisible power behind some man of influence, a Pompadour behind a throne.

218 SEVEN WOMEN AGAINST THE WORLD

In Germany, where the well-organized suffrage movement slipped unobtrusively into its own with the 'Revolution' of 1918, and where, during the Republic, there were many women in the Reichstag and the Diets of the Federal States, women have now been relegated to a position of less than secondary importance. The only institution in Germany which does not differentiate between men and women is the terror; women have been sentenced to death and executed with complete equality.

Under Hitler's régime their status has been pushed back by many generations; the higher education of women is frowned upon as it was in Europe at the beginning of the nineteenth century. Women, in the Third Realm, are considered important only as they can produce male offspring to increase the strength of the army. Hitler's Germany has not gone as far as Sparta: female infants are not destroyed at birth, but the Nazi's attitude towards them is so contemptuous that female infants are no more welcome in Germany than they were in Greece.

In the illegal revolutionary movements in Germany, as well as in Austria, however, women are particularly strong and effective at the present time. Any one with a knowledge of the German situation admits that in this crisis Germany is producing a number of really great women revolutionaries, who are, of course, forced by the terror of the Dictatorship to remain anonymous. The courage of these women is demonstrated by the enormous number of prison sentences which have been passed on many of them during the last two years.

In Russia, the earlier revolutionary women like Vera Figner or Sophie Perovskaya concentrated their efforts on overthrowing the Tsarist despotism, and they did not stop to work towards the emancipation of only one-half of the population: of women alone. In Russia, before the War, women as a whole were

IS THERE A REVOLUTIONARY TYPE? 219

more backward than they were in other European countries. Side by side with a small number of highly intellectual women there were millions of illiterates. And yet to-day in Russia, women have more complete civil and economic rights than they have in any other country in the world, the United States not excepted.

In England, where women put up the most magnificent and courageous fight for equal rights, they have attained the vote, they are citizens. But they do not enjoy economic equality. In many trades and professions they do not receive the same pay as men for the same work performed, and it may be a long time before all posts, in Government and private enterprise, will be open to them as a matter of course. So far it is considered unusual for women to hold important public posts. Appointments of women to them are heralded by the newspapers. Women still have ' news value '—their efficiency is not yet taken for granted. The fight for equal rights is not nearly over in England, and the younger generation of women would be wise to remember this fact.

For men in England are particularly bound up with the traditions of the past. Side by side with the movement for a greater equality of women, economically as well as politically, there is the subtle tradition of men, struggling, consciously or unconsciously, to keep women in what many men consider to be their place. This struggle is apparent throughout English life. If there is a son and daughter in an English family of limited means, it seems often to be taken for granted that the son shall have the University education, if only one of them can have it. The girl, so it is apparently hoped, will be successfully married off, or remain dutifully at home as an unmarried daughter. And why do some men in England speak of ' lady doctors ' when the male counterpart is not called ' gentlemen doctors ' ?

220 SEVEN WOMEN AGAINST THE WORLD

It is not by accident that men in this country have always preferred their political clubs to the *salons*, governed by women, which influenced political movements in France. Legally, women are eligible for election to the Government, they are men's equals politically, but in practice many men have not yet learned to accept them as such. Men still tend to retire to a club in Piccadilly, where politics are discussed, and women are not admitted.

Mary Wollstonecraft, probably the greatest pioneer of the emancipation of women, is listed under her husband's name in the *Encyclopædia Britannica*, that work edited by prominent men. Thus even her memory is put by them in its place. The reader may wonder to whom she was married, but his name is withheld here ; for this will prove how much better she is known than he, how ridiculous it is that future generations, and our own, studying the *Encyclopædia Britannica*, are told by men to remember her by his name.

Because of, or perhaps despite this attitude, there is no question that Englishmen are often more chivalrous towards women than are many Continentals. As an American cynically remarked, he preferred to travel on French ships in case of disaster, because, unlike the custom prevailing on British vessels, on the French boats ' there was no nonsense about women and children first.' But this chivalrousness is not enough, and during a crisis, such as the suffrage campaign, Englishmen often forgot that they were, by tradition and upbringing, chivalrous gentlemen.

Despite the somewhat condescending attitude of many men towards women's political activities, men have always been glad to accept the sacrifices of women during times of national crisis. From the days of Judith, who went forth courageously to confront

IS THERE A REVOLUTIONARY TYPE? 221

Holofernes alone, to the age of Edith Cavell when, with the utmost bravery, she stood before a German firing squad, men have not hesitated to call upon women when their country was in danger. And there have been many great women patriots, such as Boadicea or Joan of Arc, who have turned the tide of their country's fortunes.

Apart from Rosa Luxemburg, however, and a few other notable exceptions, such as Krupskaya, Lenin's widow and collaborator, and Klara Zetkin, the late veteran German feminist and revolutionary, women have as yet not been as important in the class-war as they have been in international wars. No woman has been the decisive factor finally turning the scales in favour of the revolting masses. This is surprising, for history has proven without a doubt that women are quite as courageous as men, that they are often more self-sacrificing, and that many of them are as fanatical, or more so than the men of their generation. Women, in fact, seem to derive a profound satisfaction from serving a cause. The heroism of Louise Michel was as great, or greater, than that of any of her contemporaries ; and a woman like Flora Tristan showed complete devotion to the principles for which she gave her entire strength, and ultimately her health and her life.

Since the beginning of the industrial age it is more surprising still that so few women have been the leaders of the social revolution, for women are often far more acutely aware of the injustices of the social system than are men. But they tend to see the day-to-day struggle, the personal injustices inflicted on them, rather than the deeper reasons behind them, the injustices of the system as a whole. The wife of an underpaid working man is conscious of her under-nourished children every hour of the day ; she knows how small are the supplies from which she must some-how make three meals a day, but her resentment is

222 SEVEN WOMEN AGAINST THE WORLD

often confined to an antagonism towards her husband's individual employer. And besides—and this is essential—she has no leisure and no opportunity to read or to study and thus to gain an insight into historical and social developments and movements. She often deters her husband from joining a labour movement instead of urging him to do so.

In his classic defence of women, his *Women and Socialism*, August Bebel, more than forty years ago, summed up this situation :

' From the beginning of time,' he writes, ' oppression has been the common lot of woman and labouring man. In spite of all changes in form this oppression has remained the same. Only at rare intervals during the long course of history has either woman or the labourer become alive to the consciousness of servitude, women even more rarely than men, because her position was even lower than his, and even by him she was regarded and treated as an inferior, and continues to be so to this day. Servitude which lasts for hundreds of generations ends in becoming a habit. Inheritance and education teach both parties to regard it as a natural state. Consequently woman accepts her subordinate position so entirely as a matter of course, that it costs no little effort to convince her of its degradation and to rouse in her the aspiration to become a member of society enjoying the same rights as man and to become in every respect his equal.

' That statement that from the beginning of time oppression was the common lot of woman and the labourer must be emphasized even more forcibly with regard to woman. Woman was the first human being to taste bondage. Woman was a slave before the slave existed.

' The basis of all oppression is the economic dependence on the oppressor. This has been the condition of women in the past and is still so.'

IS THERE A REVOLUTIONARY TYPE? 223

Women—that is to say, working women—have suffered a dual oppression : that imposed upon them because of their sex, and that imposed upon them by the economic discrimination against them. For the number of women belonging to the wealthy governing classes, who have unearned incomes, is extremely small as compared with the great mass of working women, whose lives are governed by the terror of unemployment, of poverty, and of want. Centuries of such oppression, furthermore, has tended to make women too meek. They do not always feel free to express their discontent even to their husbands.

Women are, in fact, frequently too patient and too fatalistic. But, despite this patience, unfortunately so general among women, it is surprising that the socialist movement has not produced a greater number of outstanding and influential women revolutionaries. It is often asked why so few women have been active in the social upheavals directed towards changing the system of society in which they live, and which oppresses them.

Why have there been so few really important women revolutionaries ?

The fact that women's oppression was indeed a dual one is, of course, one of the fundamental answers to this question. Women's strength and their ability to fight has obviously been directed largely towards their emancipation as a sex. In many countries they were—and in some countries they still are—so deeply involved in this sex-war that little energy has been left over for the class-struggle.

We often tend to forget that women have only recently begun to come into their own. The writer once saw an old will, written as late as the beginning of the nineteenth century, in which a kindly and generous husband ' left to Mathilde, his beloved wife, the silver candlesticks which her loving father gave to her as a wedding-present.'

224 SEVEN WOMEN AGAINST THE WORLD

Mathilde was undoubtedly a good and obedient wife ; her very obedience, in fact, was what made her virtuous in the judgment of the society in which she lived. For the religious traditions of all Christian countries have been and are to-day a stumbling-block to the emancipation of women, and religious prejudices are a factor to be guarded against by feminists. This is especially true, because many women themselves are naturally religious and willingly accept the inferior position assigned to them by the Church. ' Blessed are the meek ' ; but so far meek women have not inherited the earth.

The Bible gives men unlimited prestige and power ; women are told to be subservient to their husbands, fathers or brothers, at any rate, to some male. ' When a man hath taken a wife, and married her, and it come to pass that she find not favour in his eyes, because he has found some uncleanness in her ; then let him write her a bill of divorcement, and give it into her hand, and send her out of his house,' we read in Deuteronomy.

The Creator, it should be remembered in this connexion, made only man in his image and likeness ; woman—created almost as an afterthought—was nothing but a rib taken from this masterful image, and that while he slept, so that he would not suffer a moment's pain. ' And the Lord caused a deep sleep to fall upon Adam, and he slept ; and he took one of his ribs, and closed up the flesh thereof ; and the rib which the Lord God had taken from man, made he a woman, and brought her unto man.'

As this passage indicates, woman was shown less consideration than man at the very Creation : she was not granted a ' deep sleep ' when she gave birth to Adam's sons. And in the twentieth century, women are only beginning to make men realize that they are more than merely one of his own ribs, that they are indeed, a complete and independent organism, which

IS THERE A REVOLUTIONARY TYPE? 225

can move about and have its being without the assistance of men.

In no country, with the exception of Soviet Russia, is this struggle to be more than a rib, this struggle for real equality, really over. And that, as has been said, is one of the chief reasons why there have not been more outstanding women revolutionaries. Not all women, by any means, are concerned with the more far-reaching problems of society, and many of those who might dedicate their lives to the social revolution have not done so, because they are too much occupied with the emancipation of their own sex, with valiantly defending the rights which they have so far conquered.

Men are chiefly responsible for the fact that the final and complete emancipation of women has been retarded, for the world is governed by them, and nowhere in Western Europe, unfortunately, are all men civilized or enlightened. Everywhere some of them remain vaguely or more definitely antagonistic to women—as soon as women leave their homes and compete with them in the professions or on the labour market generally. Perhaps this is a primitive antagonism which will never be completely overcome. Perhaps, too, among the older generation of men, there are some who are subconsciously afraid of women, who shrink from accepting women as their equals— for fear that women might see through them. For the staunchest anti-feminists have never denied that women are ' intuitive '—though they have used this term as an argument, which seemed to them conclusive, that women are not rational creatures and have no brains. Perhaps these older men are antagonistic to women, and a little nervous, because they dimly foresee that women's strength will ultimately lie in a very dangerous combination : the combination of intuition and of brains.

This attitude shown by men to-day, when women

15

in most civilized countries have finally secured
political equality, causes women to be constantly on
the alert lest they lose their new rights. They believe
that they must continue to devote their energies to the
emancipation of their sex, for they are aware that the
realization of their political rights has not given them
economic equality. And that, after all, is the essential
factor in the emancipation of women.

Some men may have resented it when women
became their political equals, but it does not cost them
anything to allow women to vote. It might, however,
cost them a great deal if women succeeded in compet-
ing too successfully with them in business. The
average employer does not object to having his female
employee go to the polls, but he would resent it
bitterly if he had to pay her, and his other women
employees, the same wages or salaries he pays the men
in his establishment.

The leaders of the English Suffrage Movement
could not solve all the problems concerning women
at once. They had to concentrate at first on political
issues. There were women in the Suffrage Movement
of this country who were quite as heroic and as per-
severing as were any of the social revolutionary women
on the Continent. If English women had been concerned with the class-war instead of with the sex-war,
this country might have experienced a great social
upheaval.

Emily Davidson, who flung herself before the
King's horse at the Derby of 1911, died as gallantly
for her cause as Sophie Perovskaya died for hers.
Lady Constance Lytton, who died as a result of the
injuries she received in the suffrage campaign, or
Mrs. Pankhurst and her daughters, or 'General'
Drummond, or Mrs. Pethick Lawrence, or Dorothy
Evans, or 'Charlie' Marsh, or Monica Whately were
as self-sacrificing as many women revolutionaries on
the Continent. And the rank and file in the English

IS THERE A REVOLUTIONARY TYPE? 227

Suffrage Movement were as courageous as were their leaders; they suffered hunger-and-thirst strikes, they went to prison, they stood out against the rude and brutal insults of the men opposing them. These women went into battle regardless of their own safety; they used violence when necessary, though many of them hated brute force of any kind.

How ruthlessly these women themselves were treated is reflected in a statement by Hertha Ayrton, the distinguished scientist and feminist, quoted by Evelyn Sharp in her biography of Mrs. Ayrton.

After the famous meeting organized by the Women's Social and Political Union, and held in Caxton Hall, on Friday, November 18, 1910, some of the women marched up Victoria Street towards the House of Commons, where they wanted to see the Prime Minister.

'You can see from Mr. Churchill's reply in the House,' Mrs. Ayrton begins her description of this 'Black Friday,' as it was afterwards called in the Suffrage Movement, 'that the order had been given not to arrest but to wear out and terrorize the women. We heard this was so on Friday before we started, and we were not long in finding out what it meant. Before any of us, including Mrs. Pankhurst and Mrs. Garrett Anderson, could get to the House, we had to run the gauntlet of organized gangs of policemen in plain clothes, dressed like roughs, who nearly squeezed the breath out of our bodies, the policemen in official clothes helping them. When Mrs. Pankhurst and Mrs. Garrett Anderson had got through it was still worse for the rest of us. I nearly fainted, and Louie Garrett Anderson succeeded in making them let me through. Mrs. Saul Solomon was seized by the breasts and thrown down. Women were thrown from policemen in uniform to policemen in plain clothes, literally till they fainted. A lady told me a policeman had told her he would kick her when he got her down—

228 SEVEN WOMEN AGAINST THE WORLD

and he did. A man came up and said to her : ' I have been against woman's suffrage all my life, but, by God, I hope you'll get the vote now.' He said to the policeman : ' You're not a man, you're a brute.' What a libel on the brutes ! '

As this passage shows, these women in their campaign had to resort to violence ; there is no other way to meet brutality of this kind. And the admission of the fact that force was necessary—a fact proven by the Suffrage Movement in England and by every revolution in history, by every struggle for every sort of right or privilege, national or international, was an important feature of the Suffrage Movement. In this connexion it is worth remembering one of the odd contrasts in history : those individuals who want to see their country efficiently armed so that she can defend herself (with violence) against foreign enemies, are shocked by violence as such when it is applied to the class-war ; whereas people believing in a class-war—and any war is violent—disapprove of the violence of international wars.

From the beginning of the Suffrage Movement the militants were honest enough to admit that violence might occur in the sex-war as it does in any other war. The National Union of Women's Suffrage Societies, founded in 1897, advocated any methods necessary to obtain equal rights for women.

The object of the Union was ' to secure for women the Parliamentary vote as it is or may be granted to men ; to use the power thus obtained to establish equality of rights and opportunities between the sexes, and to promote the social and industrial well-being of the community.' And among the methods ' by which these objects were to be promoted,' force was included. True, the reference to this method was delicately worded, but its meaning, and the practical application of it, soon became quite clear ; the Union believed in ' vigorous agitation upon lines justified by

IS THERE A REVOLUTIONARY TYPE? 229

the position of outlawry to which women are at present condemned.'

There were many women in England who were firm believers in women suffrage, and who devoted their lives to bringing it about, but who profoundly disapproved of the violence practised by the militant members of the Union. The whole question as to whether or not violence should be applied, or whether reforms should be advocated instead, is one of the problems which, apart from their dual oppression, has prevented many women from becoming social revolutionaries. If the revolution could be carried out peacefully, if this were not a contradiction in terms, there would have been more great women revolutionaries.

By temperament, women, who are, after all, the mothers of the race, and the natural defenders of the weak, abhor violence of any kind. They have been ardent reformers ; no reformer has had a greater influence than the late Jane Addams, for instance. Women have been willing to give up their own lives, to sacrifice their own personal happiness to their work of reform. They have made tremendous and unselfish efforts to hasten the process of evolution, which would improve society. Few of these reformers, however, have been courageous enough to face the fact that reform has not been enough in most European countries, that at this point in the history of the world, now, in 1935, the oppressed can be actively helped only by a forceful upheaval. They have obtained all they can by reform.

John Stuart Mill, perhaps the greatest early advocate of women, who was the member for Westminster early in the Suffrage Movement, in the 'seventies of the last century, apparently understood women well. He recognized their pacifist-reformer instincts and talents,—and he approved of them. ' The influence of women,' he wrote, ' counts a great

230 SEVEN WOMEN AGAINST THE WORLD

deal in two of the most marked features in modern European life—its aversion to war and its addiction to philanthropy.'

This ' addiction to philanthropy ' is another reason why there have been relatively few women revolutionaries. Only unusual women, such as Vera Figner or Louise Michel, realized that to heal the wounds of humanity, without uprooting the causes of social evils, would be of no lasting value. For, as a rule, women have been satisfied to be Florence Nightingales on a large or a smaller scale. Until recently they have been inclined, passively, to let men organize and make wars, while they merely nursed the sick. They thought they were doing their whole duty if they carried baskets of food, and of flowers, to the invalid wife of one of their husband's tenants or employees, but they failed to ask why this woman was not well, to find out that perhaps she was ill because, on her husband's wages, she could not buy enough food, and that as a result of his low earnings she had overworked for years.

Women as a whole have been too enthusiastic about welfare work ; they were too often content to relieve a passing misery which happened to come within their immediate experience. They were sincere humanitarians, but they often lacked the imagination to delve into the causes which made this philanthropy necessary. In their social activities many women have been too personal.

Another reason why there have not been more women revolutionaries has been the fact that this welfare work, and the great suffrage fight, has been carried out largely by wealthy women belonging to the governing classes. Naturally, there have been notable exceptions, such as Annie Kenney, the mill-worker, who was active in the Suffrage Movement.

The Suffrage Movement did, of course, unite the women of the governing and the labouring class, but

IS THERE A REVOLUTIONARY TYPE? 231

this unity was not a permanent one, and after the Suffrage war was over, many women returned to the political parties protecting their own interests.

The temporary unity of women of all classes is reflected in a statement once made by Hertha Ayrton. 'W. T. Stead,' Mrs. Ayrton says about the first general Suffrage Congress held in London, 'was one of the speakers. He said : ' You'll never win the vote, you silken-petticoated women. You're all too damned comfortable. It will be the working women who will get it.' I have often thought of these words since the recent developments. He was not wholly right, for it is going to take the two classes together, the women of education and leisure and the wage-earning women, working side by side, to win this fight. And they are coming together now. The advent of militancy has brought about this condition. I consider that the first act of militancy, in which Christabel Pankhurst and Annie Kenney, representing the two classes of women, struck the first blow for freedom, was symbolical of this union of forces which will soon be victorious.'

Despite this co-operation, it was the ' women of education and leisure ' who had the greatest influence in the Suffrage Movement, and most of these women, who were by nature gifted as forceful revolutionaries, had no desire to change the social system. As Bebel so rightly pointed out :

'The women's question has so far been almost exclusively taken in hand by women of the upper classes, whose attention was engrossed by the limited circle in which they lived, and for whose benefits their claims were chiefly made. But the position of women in general will remain entirely unaltered whether or not some hundred or some thousand women of the needy middle classes force their way into the ranks of schoolmasters, doctors, or officials, and there secure more or less lucrative posts.'

232 SEVEN WOMEN AGAINST THE WORLD

Some of the particularly able and clear-sighted women who were active in the Suffrage Movement have now gone a step farther and are fighting for the emancipation of the oppressed of both sexes. Many of them have joined some branch of the working-class movement, for the emancipation of working women has been barely begun. Probably the most outstanding example of this type of progressive and logical women is Mrs. Despard, who became a member of the English Communist Party when she was over ninety. The Communist Party in England may be weak or it may be strong, it may be effective or it may be ineffective, but Mrs. Despard at any rate showed the courage of her convictions, she demonstrated by this step that she was profoundly concerned with all human beings who are oppressed, men as well as women, and that her valiant fight for women's suffrage was more than a personal and narrow interest in her own particular sex.

Mrs. Despard's gesture remained an example, an academic gesture, not only because this magnificent veteran has already lived the greater part of her active life. Younger women, too, cannot easily become revolutionaries in England, where there is no revolutionary movement, unless they are born leaders. This is a point often forgotten by people who wonder why there have not been more revolutionary women in this country. It would take a long time for the personalities of revolutionaries of either sex to be felt in a country where such a movement does not exist.

In England, however, one often finds *revoltées*, rebels whose rebellion is usually shortlived, whose revolt is prompted by personal dissatisfaction ; young women or men, who are revolting against the constraint of their home or their community. Their rebellion is actually the expression of their own temporary maladjustment to life. Many young women join a revolutionary movement for a brief period ; later,

IS THERE A REVOLUTIONARY TYPE? 233

when they marry and settle down, or are successful in their work and in their life, they become ordinary citizens. These *revoltées* must be mentioned here as they should never be confused with the real woman revolutionaries, who leave the security of their orderly existence to plunge themselves into that precarious no-man's-land of illegal political activities.

The attitude of serious revolutionaries is, of course, entirely different from that of these *revoltées* whose sporadic rebellion is superficial. Women revolutionaries must realize that in the present competitive system of society there can be no real economic equality for them. Only a change of the system will eventually give women exactly the same rights, political and economic, as men enjoy. It is inconceivable that any government of the present system, any capitalist country, will choose a woman as the chairman of the board of a large business or financial enterprise, or that a woman will be appointed as an Ambassador to a Great Power, or even as a Minister to a smaller country.

Naturally, men argue that women are incapable of holding such high posts or offices, for, as a whole, men have less imagination than women, and they eagerly accept this tradition as a fact. Women in Western European countries have never held these posts, so no one can say whether or not they would perform these duties as well, or better, or less efficiently than men. The feminist slogan, however, and rightly so, is ' give them a chance,' but only if the system of society is changed will this chance be given them. That is the important fact, and that is why so many women, formerly active in the feminist movements of various countries, have joined some branch of the Socialist Movement.

To work towards complete economic equality in the present system is futile. To-day, the greatest danger to the liberties and rights of women is Fascism.

Fascist countries have proven beyond a doubt that women are relegated by these dictatorships to become ' helpmates ' of man, or less, to child-bearing machines, and thus indirectly to supporters of war and terrorism. Politically, the task before all feminists—of both sexes —is to combat Fascism, to prevent this form of government from bringing about the complete collapse of all the privileges and rights for which human beings in general, and women in particular, have fought for centuries in their struggle to throw off the bondage of their dual oppression.

BIBLIOGRAPHY

Œuvres politiques de Ch. de Corday. By ' *Un Bibliophile Normand.*' Libraire Quai Voltaire, Paris, 1863.

Charlotte Corday. By Michael Corday. Thornton Butterworth, London, 1931.

Dossier Historique de Charlotte Corday. Rouquette, Paris, 1872.

Charlotte Corday ; les documents contemporains. By Henri d'Annales. Paris, 1910.

Four Frenchwomen. By Austin Dobson. Chatto & Windus, London, 1890.

Charlotte Corday. By Albert-Emile Sorel. Hachette, Paris, 1930.

Charlotte Corday, un cœur au quatre vents. By Jaques Raulet. Hachette, Paris, 1930.

Charlotte Corday : A Centenary Monograph. By Mary Jefferson. Digby, Long & Company, London, 1893.

A Woman of the Revolution : Théroigne de Méricourt. By Frank Hamel. Stanley Paul, London, 1911.

Théroigne de Méricourt. By Marcellin Pellet. Maison Quantin, Paris, 1886.

Trois Femmes de la Revolution. By Leopold Lacour. Librairie Plon, Paris, 1900.

Dr. Rigby's Letters from France in 1789. Edited by his daughter, Lady Eastlake. Longmans, Green, London, 1880.

Les Confessions de Théroigne de Méricourt. Edited by Ferdinand de Stroble-Ravelsberg. Louis Westhauser, Paris, 1892.

La Vie et l'Œuvre de Flora Tristan. By Jules L. Puech. Librarie des Sciences Sociales et Politique. Marcel Rivière, Paris, 1925.

Union Ouvrière. By Flora Tristan. Chez tous les Librairies, Paris, 1844.

Drei Jahre in Paris. By Arnold Ruge. Wilhelm Jurany, Leipzig, 1846.

236 SEVEN WOMEN AGAINST THE WORLD

Flora Tristan's Biography. By Eleanore Blanc. Chez l'auteur, Lyon, 1845.

Promenades dans Londres. By Flora Tristan. H-L. Delloye, Paris, 1840.

Louise Michel. By Irma Boyer. André Delpeuch, Paris, 1927.

Louise Michel : lavierge rouge. By Karl von Levetzow. Max Spohr, Leipzig, 1905.

La Bonne Louise. By Ernest Gurault. Bibliotheque des auteurs moderns, Paris, 1906.

Mémoires of Louise Michel. By F. Roy. Paris, 1886.

Nacht über Russland. By Vera Figner. Malik, Berlin, 1928.

Living my Life. By Emma Goldman. Knopf, New York, 1931.

Die Industrielle Entwickelung Polens. By Rosa Luxemburg. Duncker und Humbold, Leipzig, 1898.

Die Russische Revolution. By Rosa Luxemburg. Edited by Paul Levi. Verlags Gesellschaft und Erziehung G.M.B.H., 1922.

Briefe aus dem Gefägnis. By Rosa Luxemburg. Verlag der Jugendinternationale, Berlin-Schöneberg, 1922.

Briefe au Karl und Luise Kautsky. By E. Laub'sche Verlagsbuchhandlung, Berlin, 1923.

Die Russische Revolution. Edited by Paul Levi. Verlag Gesellschaft und Erziehung, Berlin, 1922.

Rosa Luxemburg. By Luise Kautski. E. Laub'sche Verlagsbuchhandlung, Berlin, 1929.

Die Akkumulation des Kapitals. By Rosa Luxemburg. Buchhandlung Vorwärts Paul Singer G.M.B.H., Berlin, 1913.